HANDY REFERENCE

<HEAD>..</HEAD>	Contains head area
<TITLE>..</TITLE>	Title (on top line)
<BASE HREF=...>	Base URL
<META>..</META>	Document information
<BODY>..</BODY>	Contains body area
<ADDRESS>..</ADDRESS>	Author's details
<P>..</P>	Paragraph
<UL>..</UL>	Unordered list
<OL>..</OL>	Ordered list
<LI>	List item
<DL>..</DL>	Definition list
<DT>	Data term
<DD>	Data definition
<PRE>..</PRE>	Preformatted text
<DIV>..</DIV>	Text division
<CENTER>..</CENTER>	Centred text
<BLOCKQUOTE>..</BLOCKQUOTE>	Indented quote
<FORM>..</FORM>	Fill-in form
<INPUT>	Input field
<SELECT>..</SELECT>	Menu
<OPTION>	Item in menu
<TEXTAREA>..</TEXTAREA>	Multi-line text input
<TABLE>..</TABLE>	Table
<CAPTION>..</CAPTION>	Table caption
<TR>..</TR>	Table row
<TH>..</TH>	Header cell
<TD>..</TD>	Data cell
<H1>..</H1>	Heading 1 (biggest)
<H6>..</H6>	Heading 6 (smallest)
<B>..</B>	Bold text
<I>..</I>	Italic text
<TT>..</TT>	Teletype text
<U>..</U>	Underline text
<STRIKE>..</STRIKE>	Strikeout text
<BIG>..</BIG>	Big text
<SMALL>..</SMALL>	Small text
_{..}	Subscript text
^{..}	Superscript text
<EM>..</EM>	Emphasis
<STRONG>..</STRONG>	Strong text
<FONT>..</FONT>	Font size
<BASEFONT>	Base font size
<HR>	Horizontal rule
 	Line break
<!-- ... -->	Comment
<DFN>..</DFN>	Definition
<CODE>..</CODE>	Program code
<SAMP>..</SAMP>	Sample output
<KBD>..</KBD>	Keyboard Input
<VAR>..</VAR>	Variables
<CITE>..</CITE>	Citations
<A>..</A>	Hypertext anchor
<IMG>	Image
<MAP>	Image map table
<APPLET>..</APPLET>	Java Applet
<PARAM>	Java parameter
<SCRIPT>..</SCRIPT>	Javascript code
<EMBED>..</EMBED>	Plug-In

ABOUT THE SERIES

In easy steps series is developed for time-sensitive people who want results fast. It is designed for quick, easy and effortless learning.

By using the best authors in the field, combined with our in-house expertise in computing, this series is ideal for all computer users. It explains the essentials simply, concisely and clearly - without the unnecessary verbal blurb. We strive to ensure that each book is technically superior, effective for easy learning and offers the best value.

Learn the essentials **in easy steps** - accept no substitutes!

Titles in the series include:

Operating Systems

Windows 95	1-874029-28-8

Applications - Integrated

Microsoft Office	1-874029-37-7
Microsoft Office 97	1-874029-66-0
Microsoft Works	1-874029-41-5
SmartSuite	1-874029-67-9

Applications - General

Access	1-874029-57-1
Excel	1-874029-69-5
PowerPoint	1-874029-63-6
Word	1-874029-39-3
Word 97	1-874029-68-7
WordPerfect	1-874029-59-8

Accounting and Finance

Microsoft Money UK	1-874029-61-X
Quicken UK	1-874029-71-7
Sage Instant Accounting	1-874029-44-X
Sage Sterling for Windows	1-874029-43-1

Internet

CompuServe UK	1-874029-33-4
FrontPage	1-874029-60-1
HTML	1-874029-46-6
Internet Explorer	1-874029-58-X
Internet UK	1-874029-31-8
Netscape Navigator	1-874029-47-4

Graphics and Desktop Publishing

CorelDRAW	1-874029-72-5
PageMaker	1-874029-35-0
PagePlus	1-874029-49-0
Publisher	1-874029-56-3

For credit card sales and volume discounts Tel: 01926 817999 or EMail: sales@computerstep.com

For international orders and rights Fax: +44 1926 817005 or EMail: sevanti@computerstep.com

EMail your reader comments to: harshad@computerstep.com

Visit our web site at http://www.computerstep.com

HTML in easy steps

Andy Holyer

In easy steps is an imprint of Computer Step
Southfield Road . Southam
Warwickshire CV33 OFB . England

Tel: 01926 817999 Fax: 01926 817005
http://www.computerstep.com

First published 1997

Notice of Liability
Every effort has been made to ensure that this book contains accurate and current information. However, Computer Step and the author shall not be liable for any loss or damage suffered by readers as a result of any information contained herein.

Trademarks
Microsoft and Windows are registered trademarks of Microsoft Corporation. All other trademarks are acknowledged as belonging to their respective companies.

Printed and bound in the United Kingdom

ISBN 1-874029-46-6

Contents

CHAPTER ONE

First Steps

This chapter describes the World-Wide Web, looks at some of the different types of sites which can be found there, and explains what you'll need to go about creating your own web site.

Covers

Introduction

For new users of the Internet, by far the most-used service is the World-Wide Web – indeed, many people never use anything else. After a few months of browsing the web, you may want to set up your own web page. This is the need which this book addresses.

There are many reasons why you may want to produce a web page. You may just want a personal page, letting other web users know about you and your family. You may have a small business which you want to advertise, or you may have more ambitious plans. This book can help you with all of these desires to some degree or another.

If you don't yet have an Internet connection, read the book "Internet UK in easy steps", published by Computer Step.

A small amount of initial knowledge is assumed on the part of the reader. You should have access to a personal computer with Internet access, and should have a basic ability with handling an Internet connection. However, you don't need previous knowledge of programming. HTML can be viewed as a programming language (though a fairly simple one), but anyone capable of using a word processor can produce a web page. Some more advanced elements of web design do need programming experience, in particular CGI scripts and Java – though you can "borrow" existing code and tailor it to your own needs.

Besides a copy of a World-Wide Web browser, no other software is actually necessary. It is entirely possible to produce a sophisticated web presence using nothing more elaborate than Windows Notepad and a few Internet tools. From time to time other applications may be useful, and pointers will be provided as to where you can get these if you wish.

There are now available elaborate HTML design tools. Many professional web site designers never use them, but it's up to you. Tools make it much easier to control the layout of your site, and they can speed up the production of pages, but at the end of the day you need to have a thorough grasp of the underlying HTML to produce a really good page, and that is what most space will be devoted to here.

What do you need?

You will need access to a personal computer with, as a minimum, a web browser and editing facilities. There are a number of commercial web authoring packages available: these can be useful, but they're not essential. You'll also need access to the Internet to put your site on-line.

As long as your machine is powerful enough to run the necessary software, it doesn't need to be a very high specification. Obviously it would be very nice to have a 200Mhz Pentium Pro with plenty of memory and disk space: but it's entirely possible (though a bit frustrating) to develop a web page on a fairly old machine – I know of one person who manages on a 386SX machine with 2Mb of memory.

The examples used in this book are based on someone using a PC running Windows: however, most of the information is valid even if you use a Macintosh or a Unix workstation. As long as you can run a web browser and can generate text and image files on your chosen computer, you'll be able to use the information in this book.

There is then the issue of actually putting the pages you have produced onto the World Wide Web. It is generally too expensive to have your own web server – you need a dedicated computer, and some sort of high-speed connection to the Internet. This is likely to cost at least £10,000 per year. Fortunately, most Internet Service Providers will rent out web space. You will need to arrange this, and will also probably need an account with a provider to place your pages on the site. This doesn't have to be with the same provider as you rent space with, but it's often easier if it is.

Assuming you're using web space on a commercial server, you don't even need that powerful a modem: web sites don't take up much memory, and you only need to transfer them to the server once, so a 14.4 or a 28.8 modem is quite sufficient to install a site. That's not to say that a 33.6 isn't nice, though.

The Internet

The Internet is a worldwide network of computers, linked together using telephone lines. The origins of the Internet lie in the Cold War. A plan was devised to connect up military computers spread around the United States, so that in case of nuclear attack the US military machine would still be able to operate. These machines were linked together using telephone lines. The first two machines were connected up at the end of 1969.

For the first 15 years of its life, almost the only sites connected were military and academic. There were a number of networks set up, including ARPAnet, which connected US universities, and MILnet, which connected up military bases. The first UK system linked up five UK universities in the late seventies. This grew into the UK academic network, JANET.

In the 1980s the various networks began to be linked together, so you could get from one network to another. This is when the name "Internet" was first coined.

At around the same time, public access Internet service providers began to appear. There are now over 200 Internet service providers in the United Kingdom alone, ranging from national services to small local or special-interest providers. Despite its origins, the Internet has proved to have mainly peaceful uses. Until about 1990, it was dedicated to scientific research, especially in high-energy physics and space science. The dominance of the scientific community on the Internet is beginning to erode, however, as members of the public come to realise the potential it has as a means of global communication, entertainment and education. Today there are over 40 million people connected to the Internet around the world, in virtually every country.

The World-Wide Web

The biggest advance in ease of use for the Internet was when Tim Berners-Lee invented the World-Wide Web in the early 1990s. Tim was working at the time at the CERN high-energy physics laboratory in Switzerland, where they had particular needs for exchanging information: a worldwide population of researchers (scientists only visit CERN for a few weeks at a time – most of the work is done from their home labs), and the need to share a wide variety of different types of data, including graphs and raw data from scientific instruments.

Tim's solution was to design a simple, easy-to-extend scripting language called HTML (HyperText Markup Language). HTML allowed a variety of different types of data to be integrated seamlessly, and allowed links between data situated anywhere on the Internet.

Although it was quite well received, the WWW was only one of a number of similar projects on the Internet at that time. The real breakthrough came when Marc Andreeson (then of the University of Illinois, now chief executive of Netscape) wrote a World-Wide Web browser called Mosaic.

You can download Mosaic from http://www.ncsa.uiuc.edu.

For the first time there was a way to access the Internet which could be used without having to learn to operate a complicated command-line interface. Mosaic also provided a colourful and interesting interface to the Internet.

Mosaic was later superseded by Netscape Navigator as the main browser (see page 13), and more recently Microsoft Internet Explorer (see opposite) has also started to dominate this market.

HyperText

The most technically-important element which the World-Wide Web provided was not the visual aspect: it was the use of HyperText.

The term HyperText was coined by a man called Alan Kay working at Xerox research labs in the early 1970s. Kay developed a number of innovations in computer interfaces during this period, many of which are now commonplace. These include the mouse, and the Windows-Icons-Desktop system familiar to users of the Apple Macintosh and of Windows. None of these innovations were used by Xerox at the time: many of them have since been exploited by others.

HyperText is a difficult concept to explain, but quite an easy one to understand. A good comparison is with books. You read most books by starting at the beginning, going on until you get to the end, and then stopping. You would never read a reference book this way (unless you have a *very* dull life, of course). What you'd do is go straight to the item you wanted to know about. Each item has references to other items which are related to it, and you look up the ones which interest you. These in turn have references and you can carry on following references for as long as you want. There's no guarantee, however, that you will ever get to every item in the book this way.

HyperText works like a reference book. Each World-Wide Web "page" can have links to other pages. You go to these "hyperlinks" by clicking on them with your mouse. One refinement which the World-Wide Web provides (unlike a CD-ROM, for example) is that these links can be anywhere on the Internet, so your pages in England can connect more-or-less seamlessly to your friend's pages in Australia. This explains the "Web" part of the World-Wide Web.

Web browsers

The program you use to look at the World-Wide Web is called a "browser". There are a number of different browsers available, most of them for download from the Internet. Your Internet service provider should supply you with a browser when you sign up.

Most of the time it doesn't really matter which browser you use – try a couple and settle on the one you're most comfortable with. For the really advanced features of the web, you'll need to be running the latest version of either Netscape Navigator or Microsoft Internet Explorer (you'll need a pretty powerful machine, too). The latest versions change every few weeks, but don't worry too much if you're not 100% up to date; you'll still be able to view most of the web quite OK.

Before you start producing web pages, you should be quite happy working a World-Wide Web browser. It's not really the place of this book to explain how to work a browser – read "Netscape Navigator in easy steps" or "Internet Explorer in easy steps" if you need some help with that.

It's important to test your pages using a browser before you let them out on the Internet. If possible, try them out using several different browsers. If you can try different types of machines (PC, Macintosh, Workstation), all the better. But you'll look smarter if the person who finds the page that doesn't work is you, not some 15-year-old in Texas.

Tools to help you

It is possible to produce a professional web site using nothing more than Windows Notepad to produce HTML, and Paint to prepare images. In fact, a lot of professional web authors do use Notepad for the HTML.

Alternatively, there is a range of what-you-see-is-what-you-get HTML editors, ranging from freeware editors, to products like Microsoft FrontPage.

HANDY TIP

You can download a demo version of FrontPage from http://www.microsoft.com/frontpage.

FrontPage has some advantages: the visual representation of how pages link together is good; it's especially good for a team of people to work collectively on more than one web site; and there are wizards to help you set up the more common type of site – but in ordinary HTML preparation, it's not a lot faster than using Notepad, in my opinion.

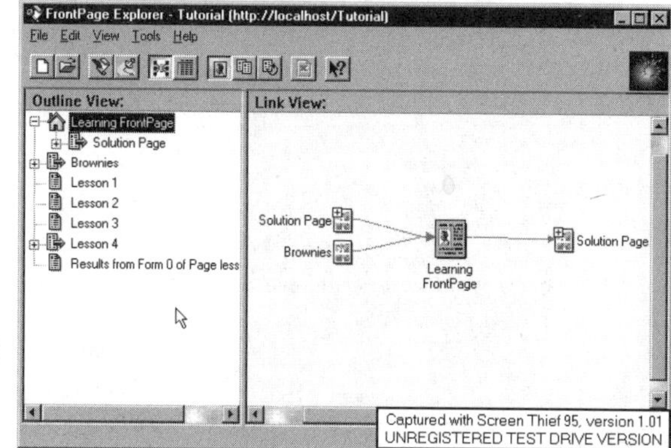

Another option you may consider is that there are now extensions from a number of word-processing and desktop publishing applications which allow you to export a document in HTML format: the resulting web pages will as near as possible resemble the page as displayed in the application. For example, Word has a module to allow documents to be saved as HTML, and there is a Quark Xpress Xtension for the same purpose. You need to have bought a copy of the relevant application (and with Quark costing over £500 this is no small step), but if you've already got documents which you wish to transfer onto the web (for example, a product catalogue), this approach may be useful to you.

You will also need an application to edit images. At the simplest level, this can be Windows Paint, but it's well worth opting for something more sophisticated. If you're rich (or it came with a scanner) Adobe Photoshop is about the best thing, but there is a range of packages available, some of them for download from the Internet. There are a few details of image generation which web pages require but which mainstream applications don't handle – for example, producing multiple-image GIF files, or generating image maps. There are dedicated freeware or shareware applications available for this on the Internet to do these sorts of things, and these will be covered as we need them.

However, the growing popularity of web-page design has seen the arrival of a number of all-in-one graphics packages with web facilities, such as PhotoImpact. This is designed to integrate with the Microsoft Office suite, though you don't really need Office to use it, and it now incorporates many new features specifically designed for web page authors. For example, it lets you easily create attractive backgrounds for your pages, allows you to design colourful, ornamented hot-link buttons, and provides easy ways to align all the objects on a page just as you want them, without having to bother with the underlying HTML codes. One particularly striking feature is the Frame & Shadow designer, which lets you create distinct framed areas on your pages, and give drop shadows even to irregularly shaped objects.

Lastly, you need to have installed the most recent version of your favourite web browser, and if possible the latest versions of other browsers as well. This lets you try out your pages, to make sure they look OK when you put them on the web. You should try a range of browsers because even if they say they conform to the standard, in practice there are subtle differences in the way different browsers lay out the same page. If you can, it's an idea to have an older version of a browser around as well – not everyone runs the latest version of software, and it's always disappointing to discover that your favourite gimmick is spoilt because (say) an old version of Netscape Navigator won't handle it correctly.

Some typical sites

Here are some examples of the sort of web page you may want to produce.

The Home page

This is Tom Shepard's Home page. Tom is an A-Level student living in Brighton, who is keen to be a journalist. His page gives examples of articles he has written, and tells you about his interests, and links to pages that he likes. It also has a photo of his girlfriend in there somewhere.

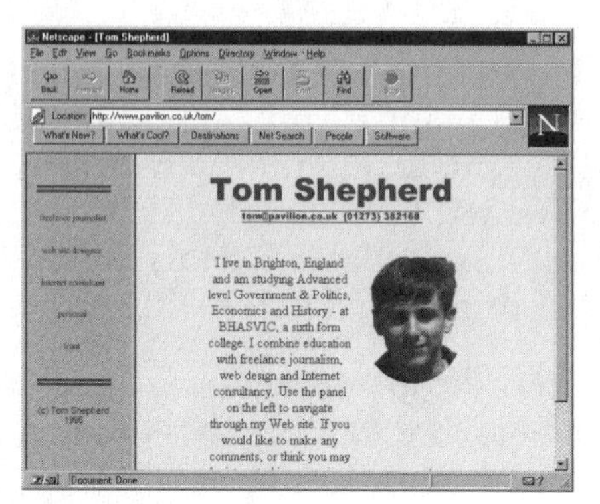

The personal home page is the first thing that many Internet users put on the web. You have had an Internet account for a few months, and have made a few friends on Newsgroups and IRC channels. Now you want to let your new friends know what you look like.

A home page rarely takes up more than a megabyte or two of memory, so it's a cheap way to dip your toe in the water. Many Internet service providers allow you a small allocation for a home page as part of your subscription.

The small business

This is the home page of W.E. Baxter, a long-established family printing firm from Lewes in Sussex. The home page gives information about the services Baxter's can provide, and allows potential customers to contact the company by eMail.

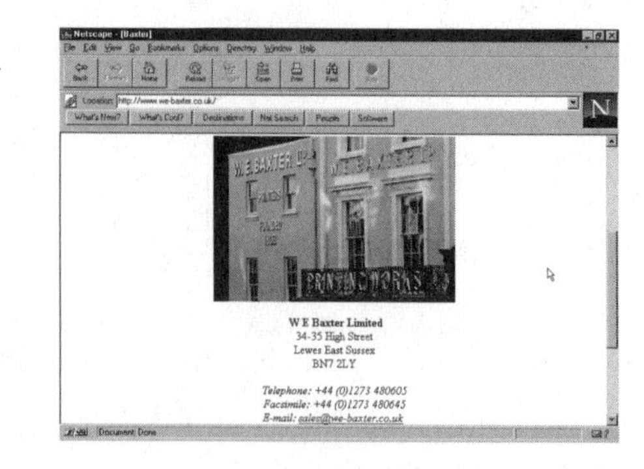

If you own or work for a small company, it is quite possible for you to produce a home page of this type. There is no great need for exotic HTML tricks, and unless you have an extensive catalogue it should not take more than a couple of megabytes of web space – possibly it will even fit in the free allocation which some Internet service providers allow you.

The high-profile site

This is the web page of Diesel Jeans, the Italian high-fashion label. The site has won a number of awards from magazines and on-line services.

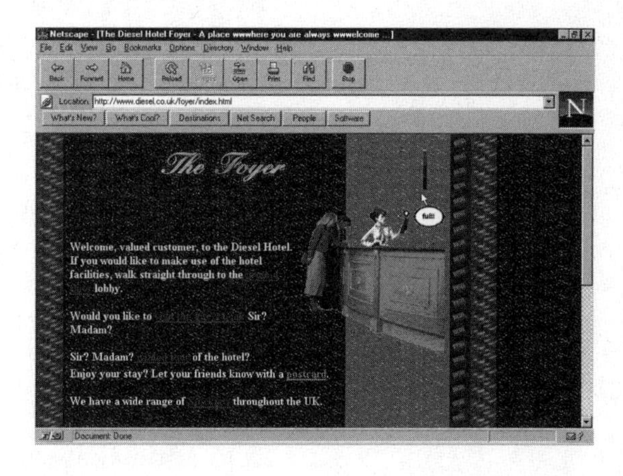

Essentially the site is Diesel's advertising campaign and catalogue converted into a web site.

A site like this has a budget of thousands of pounds, but it was put together using similar methods and equipment to those that are covered in this book.

Is your page really necessary?

Before you throw yourself into the process of designing and developing your web page, it's well worth devoting a bit of time to thinking about your page, and what it should do.

Whether you are producing a page for a company, or just a home page for yourself, this is important. In the case of a personal page, too many home pages start out neatly enough, but then fizzle out after a bit into a maze of "under construction" links. Don't fall into this trap: if you are too impatient to finish your page covering your top 50 films, don't think you'll go back and finish it when you've got time, because believe me, you won't. I know: I've done it myself. *Nothing* looks worse than a half-finished home page.

If you're producing a home page for a small business or for an organisation, take a while to make sure that the page you're producing really adds something to the Internet as a whole, and that people will have a reason to visit it (and to come back again later).

In the last year or so, having your own web page has become very fashionable, and the most extraordinary companies have set up presences on the web. A large percentage of these sites provide no more information than a magazine advertisement or a handbill. Others are just not suited to the Internet. The worst offender I recall was a site for an undertakers. Maybe I'm just odd, but I've never had a great desire to order coffins by mail order, and if I were recently bereaved, the last thing I'd be interested in would be surfing the 'Net.

This advice applies just as much to large companies who have spent thousands of pounds on their servers.

An example of a good angle for a site is Vauxhall's web site. The site provides a catalogue of the Vauxhall range (like most motor manufacturer sites) but in addition provides a service called "Traffic Net". This displays the average speed of traffic on a section of UK motorways, and the information is updated live as you watch. This approach encourages people to come back to the site more than once.

Another interesting angle is the Carling Black Label site. This has nothing to do with beer at all, but is based upon the fact that Carling are the sponsors of the Premier League. The CarlingNet site has been set up to be the definitive football site in the UK. There are details of every league club, with links to any web pages they may have, a complete results listing, and a quite nice set of discussion groups, one per club. And not a beer can in sight. I like this site a lot, even though I don't follow football or drink lager.

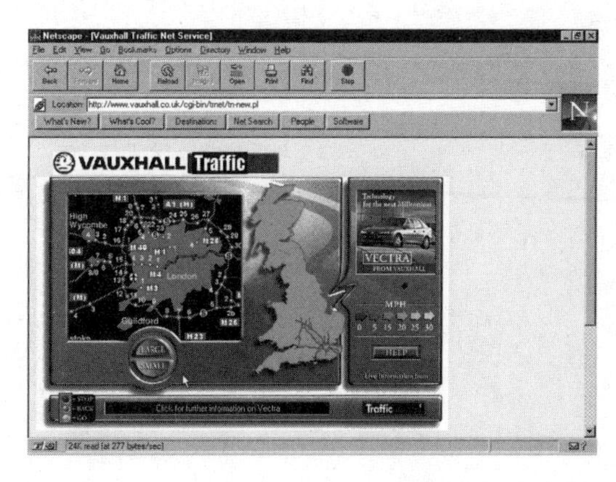

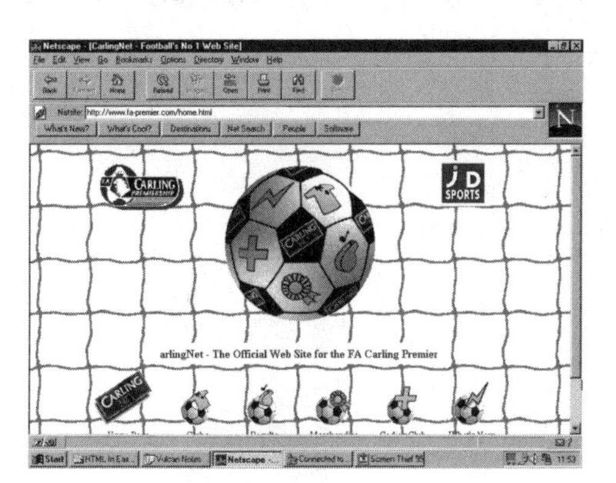

Straightforward selling sites do work, but only if the product satisfies certain criteria. First of all, it must appeal to the average Internet user – and despite advances, most people on the Internet are male, aged between 16 and 35, and keen on technology. Secondly, it should be easy to sell the product world-wide, or at least nationwide. There are a couple of excellent US sites selling mail-order CDs, but you'll probably find that once you've added on postage, duty and exchange costs it would work out cheaper to buy the music locally.

A better idea for a commercial site is this one, which sells hot chillies and hot sauces. This is another interest which I'm afraid has simply passed me by, but if you like highly-spiced foods, you will find more types of hot sauce than you would ever imagine, all available by mail order world-wide quite cheaply. There is no way that a shop which just sold hot sauces would make a profit anywhere in the world, but via this web page, they get a world audience of Internet users (a lot of whom *do* like hot food) and can sell to them relatively cheaply.

CHAPTER TWO

URLs

The World-Wide Web identifies resources using a scheme called a "Uniform Resource Locator". This chapter explains how to read a URL.

Covers

Why use a URL?

One of the nice things with the World-Wide Web is that it does not distinguish between a file which is on your local computer, one which is on your local-area network, or one anywhere else on the Internet. It can also handle a range of Internet protocols, other than its own HyperText Transfer Protocol. To allow this to happen, it defines a notation called a Uniform Resource Locator, or URL for short.

The URL gives you three items of information: a "service descriptor" which specifies the protocol to use; the Internet address at which the file can be found; and the place on that service where the file is located.

Every file which is accessible on the Internet has a URL, and could in principle be referenced from any document on the World-Wide Web. It is this uniformity of access which gives the web its universal appearance.

A URL has the same format regardless of what operating system the server uses. A file which on a Unix system would be described as "/pub/file.htm" would on a Windows machine be "\pub\file.htm"; on a Macintosh the same location would be written ":pub:file.htm", and older operating systems would use different formats for essentially the same information. The URL standard makes all of these different notations the same.

How to read a URL

A typical URL will look like this:

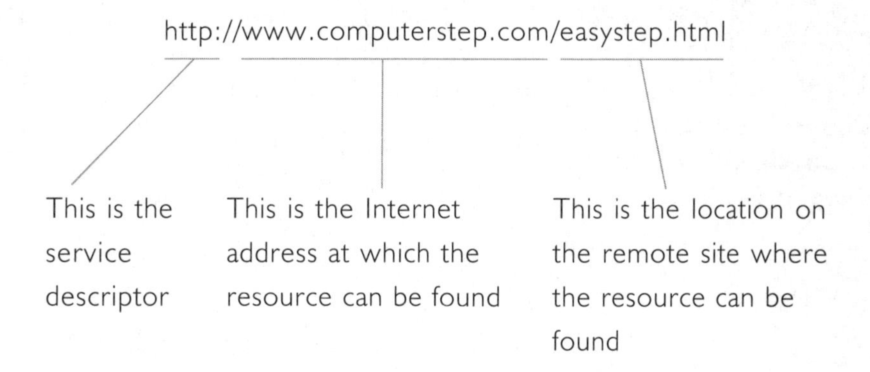

A few service types don't follow this pattern exactly. A mailto: URL looks like this:

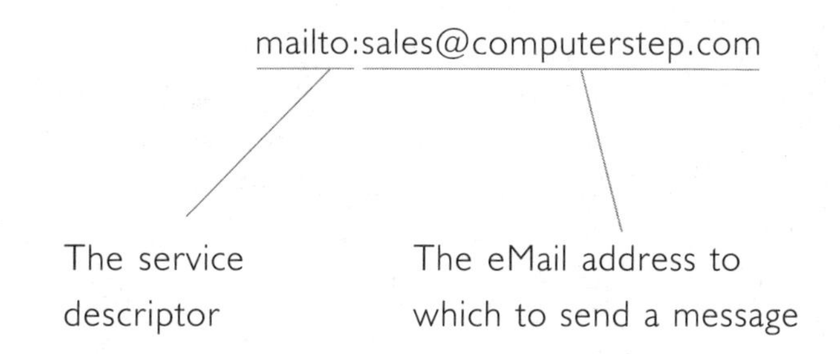

Entering this URL into your web browser would launch your eMail editor, and allow you to send a message. See the following two pages for more information on service types and Internet addresses.

Service types

A protocol describes the method used to access a particular Internet service.

The first part of the URL describes the Internet protocol which the browser should use to fetch the resource.

The most common service found on the World-Wide Web is **http:**, which specifies HyperText Transfer Protocol, the protocol used by World-Wide Web servers.

A variation on http: is **https:**, which specifies a secure HTTP connection. Between a suitable browser and server this allows the connection to be encrypted. This is useful if sensitive information (like credit card numbers, for example) is being exchanged.

Another common service is **ftp:**. This tells the browser to open an anonymous FTP connection to the site stated, and to fetch the file. If you want to use ftp: links, you must have an FTP server set up to handle anonymous connections. Most commercial web space providers have this facility.

A **mailto:** URL tells the browser to open a window to send an eMail to the address specified. The user is presented with a blank window in which to compose a message. Some browsers open their own window: others (like Internet Explorer) use your normal eMail package.

It's one of those annoying elements of HTML that there's no easy way to specify the subject of the message, or fill in any of its contents. It would be nice if this was possible but it isn't – yet.

A **telnet:** URL tells the browser to use your telnet application (assuming you have one) to open a telnet connection to the address specified. Telnet is a character-based connection which looks a bit like a DOS shell. Unless you're doing something very technical, or are into MUDs, you'll probably never need to use this.

Finally, a **news:** URL tells the browser to fetch the newsgroup stated from the local news server. Note that this will probably not be your local server, so you can't guarantee that any particular article can be found.

Internet addresses

The Internet address part of a URL tells the browser where to fetch the resource described.

Internet addresses can be expressed in two ways. The normal way (which you should use whenever possible) is using a domain name.

Internet domain names consist of a series of domains separated by dots. The least significant domain is on the left; the most significant is on the right. For example:

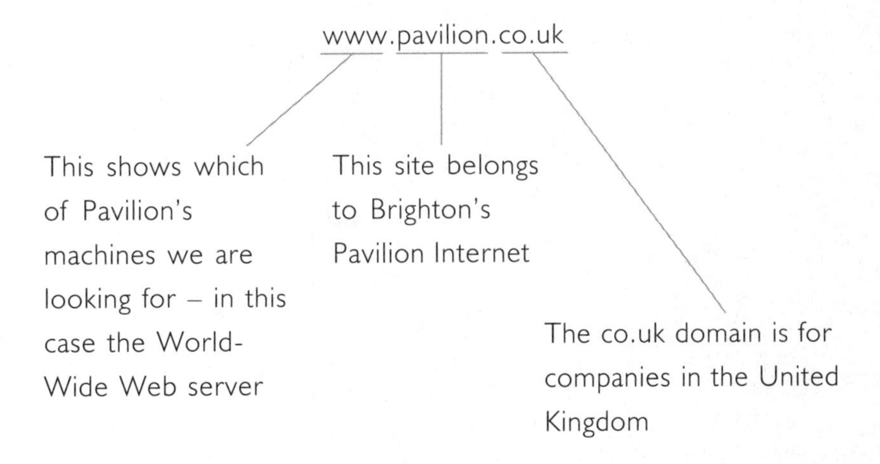

Internet domain names are converted by the software into the way they are handed internally, which is in the form of a number. This number is usually expressed as a series of four numbers between 0 and 255, each separated by dots – for example,

158.152.164.54

This is called a "tuple" (never mind why). You can construct a URL using a tuple instead of a domain name, but for a number of boring technical reasons it's not a good idea. Always use a domain name where possible.

Port addressing

The Internet address discussed on the previous page determines which computer on the Internet to contact. We still need to determine which program running on that machine to contact. This is done using ports.

An Internet request can be addressed to one of 65536 possible ports on the destination machine (only a few ports are usually used). A World-Wide Web server, for example, usually responds to requests to port 80, and a normal **http:** URL will be addressed to this port.

Sometimes you may wish to send a request to an unusual port – for example if there is an experimental web server on a site, which may be set up to use a different port. To indicate the alternative port, put the port number on the end of the Internet address, separated by a colon.

Since these temporary web servers are... well, temporary, an example that is valid today won't be valid tomorrow. So: suppose that we've got a temporary web server at the (fictional) University of Dorset, on port 8080 (for some reason, that's a common port for temporary web servers). The URL for this site would be:

http://www.dorset.ac.uk:8080/

You can use the same notation for other URLs. This is most useful in the case of **telnet:** URLs.

The pathname

The rest of the URL after the Internet address is referred to as the "pathname", and says where on the remote server the file can be found.

The first slash after the address indicates the "root" of the web server. You can set up where this is on the host machine when you set up the web server, to ensure that any other files on the machine cannot be accessed on the World-Wide Web.

There then may follow one or more directories and then the file name. This is just like a DOS pathname, with one exception: instead of a backslash, "\" (which you'd have in DOS), use a forward slash, "/" which is what a Unix machine uses.

You do not have to put a filename on the end of a URL. If the URL ends with a "/" the web server will look in the relevant directory to see if there is an index file. The name of this file depends on the web server: usually it is called "index.html", but some servers also recognise "welcome.html", and it is also possible to set this up for an individual server.

If the index file exists, this is displayed. If not, a listing of the contents of the directory is displayed. Since you usually don't want outsiders poking around amongst the actual files, it's a good idea to make sure that all the directories on your server have an index file.

In general, names in a pathname are case-sensitive: "fred" is different from "Fred", which is also different from "FRED". Be careful about this if you develop on a Windows 3.1 computer. Also, it's not a good idea to have spaces in path or file names, but if you do, they should be converted to "+" signs in the URL.

Virtual servers

Usually, if you rent space on a commercial server, you will be given access to a directory on their server, and your URL will reflect that fact. So, the root URL of your server will be something like:

http://www.website.co.uk/Users/mysite/

You may not want to do this, especially if you're setting up a commercial site – you want people to think that you've spent enough to set up your own site.

Most commercial providers provide this service, which is described as a "virtual server". By tweaking the setup of their web server, they make it look as if you've got your own server – that is:

It is possible for a really clever user to find out that you're using a virtual server rather than a real one.

http://www.mysite.co.uk/

...will point to your area on their server. This is all an illusion – you don't really have your own server, but it's a lot cheaper than having your own dedicated machine.

An example of a company providing virtual web hosting in this way is Virtual Internet Limited. You can check their details and prices at:

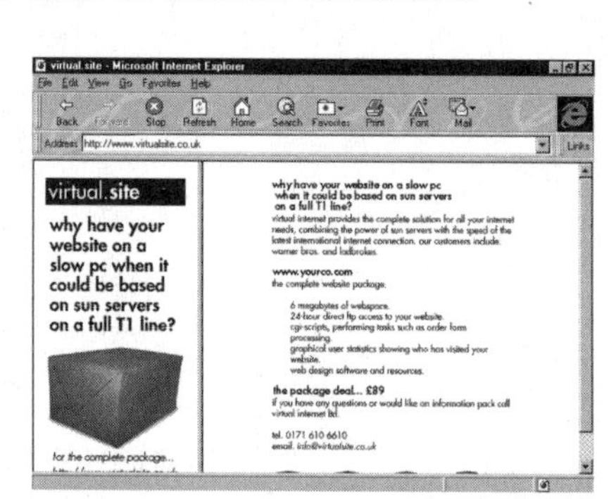

http://www.virtualsite.co.uk/

They can also register your domain name (see http://www.desig.net) with the relevant authorities: for example, via Nominet (http://www.nic.uk) for .co.uk domains or via Internic in the USA (http://www.internic.net) for international commercial companies requiring domain names to end with .com. There is a separate annual subscription fee to keep the registration.

CHAPTER THREE

Basic HTML

This chapter goes through the basic syntax of HTML. When you have finished this chapter you will know enough to produce simple web pages.

Covers

Overview

Let's get the boring technical bit out of the way first: HTML is a Data Type Descriptor (DTD) of Standard Generalised Mark-Up Language (SGML). SGML is an international standard which describes how to take text stored on computer, and mark it up to add extra information, in the same way as a proof reader used to mark up a printed page. SGML is the basic scheme for all kinds of mark-up that anyone could possibly want. A DTD specifies the exact types of mark-up that should be used for a particular purpose. In case you're interested, other SGML DTDs allow text to be marked up to allow computerised translation (so that words can be tagged as a noun or a verb, for example), or to annotate a text (like the editions of Shakespeare which have a glossary, for instance). Now you know what a DTD is. Now you can forget it again.

Because of the success of the World-Wide Web, the commonest SGML DTD is HyperText Markup Language, which is the reason we're here.

The core of any HTML document is just text. The text is marked up using HTML tags. Tags look like this:

HANDY TIP

Tags can be in either upper or lower case (or even in mixed case). I tend to write tags in capitals, since it makes them easier to spot.

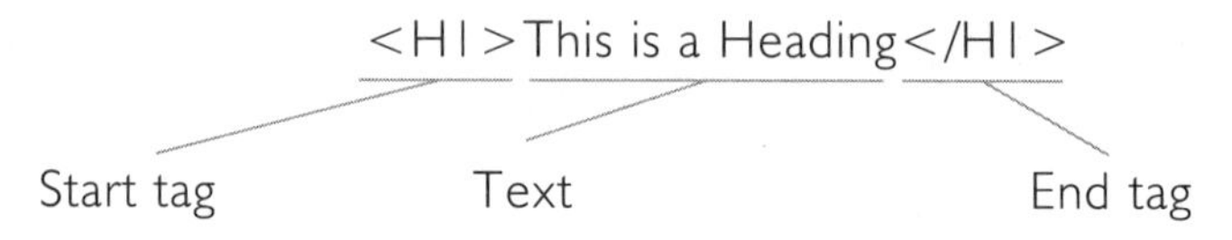

All HTML tags come between a "<" and a ">". Most tags affect an area of text, and come in pairs. If a start tag is "<TAG>", the end tag will be "</TAG>". All the mark-up information you provide to the browser comes from some type of tag.

Some types of tag need extra information. For example, an IMG tag (which produces an inline image) needs the filename of the image, and possibly information about the size of the image and how the browser should align the image with respect to the surrounding text. This information is called the tag's "attributes". Only start tags have attributes – they're meaningless in an end tag. Attributes look like this:

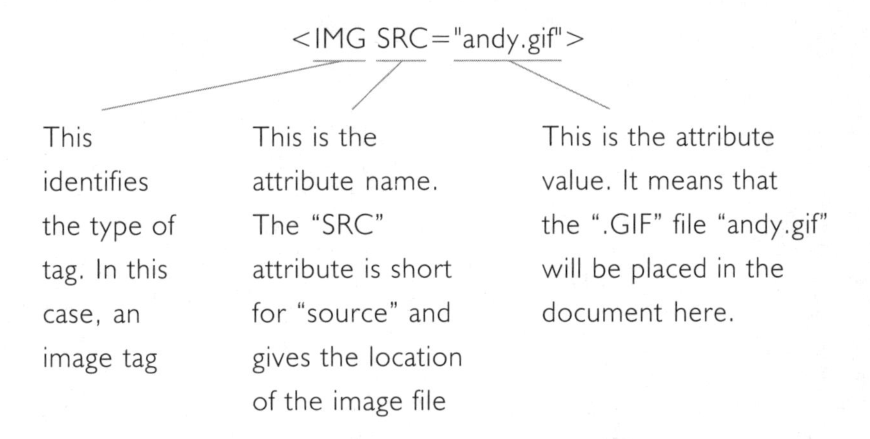

Some types of tags need a number of attributes. That's easy: just put one or more spaces (or tabs, or new lines) between each attribute-value pair. Attribute names, like tags, can be written in either capitals or lower case (or in a mixture of both, if you really want to). Most attribute values *are* case-sensitive (that is, if your file is called "andy.gif" and you write "Andy.gif" in your HTML file, it won't work). You don't always *have* to put attribute values in quotes, but it can be a good idea. If the value has spaces in it then you do have to use quotes.

REMEMBER

"Semantics" means what the page actually means, rather than what it physically looks like.

An important thing to remember when you're producing HTML is that it only specifies the *semantics* of the page: the actual layout is up to the browser – for example, what font is used for display, or what font size to use. You can get round this to a degree by using style sheets (on some browsers, at least), but generally you should not rely on your page looking exactly like it does on your computer. We'll come back to this concept later on.

Versions of HTML

HTML was originally designed as a small, simple set of tags which could be learned in an afternoon and was satisfactory for most purposes. As is the way of such things, however, soon people were coming up with extensions. The result of this is that there is a bewildering range of versions of HTML around.

The worst offenders are the manufacturers of browsers. They are keen to show off the clever things that their own browser can do and which the others can't, so they produce their own set of extensions to HTML. Some of these extensions do useful things, and some of them have now been adopted by "official" HTML. The problem with all this is that if you use their set of extensions, you've got no guarantee that someone looking at your page will be using that particular browser. If they don't have the right software, they won't see your page as you intended them to see it, and some of the effect is lost.

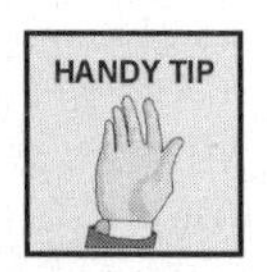

You can always find the latest definition of the HTML standard (and other useful information) on the W3 web site at http://www.w3.org.

"Standard" HTML is defined by the "W3 Organisation", which is based at the MIT in Boston, USA. If you keep to their standards, then you've got a pretty good chance that most browsers on the Internet will be able to view your page. The most recent version is 3.2, which is the standard which will be used for most of this book.

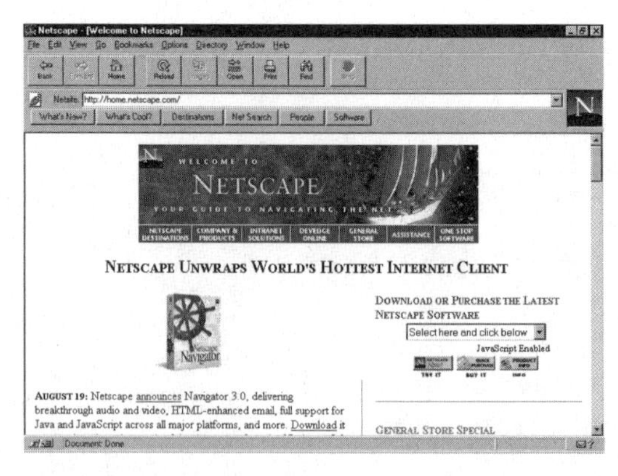

The two main sets of proprietary extensions are produced by the two leading producers of commercial browsers. Netscape corporation were the worst offenders in adding extensions in the early days of the web. They still do it, but fortunately most of their extensions have now become part of the official standard. For the time being, Netscape

Navigator is still the market leader in browsers, so if you use Netscape extensions you've got a fair chance of your pages being viewed by a large audience.

Internet Explorer often turns up on magazine cover CDs. If you can't find it, you can download it from http://www.microsoft.com/ie.

The main competitor for Netscape is Microsoft's Internet Explorer. Until recently, Explorer was by far an inferior browser to Netscape Navigator: the only real reason to use it (besides the fact that it came free with every copy of Windows) was that it was smaller than Netscape, so it would run faster on a low-spec machine. Microsoft's new version of Explorer (version 4) is very impressive. When you consider the number of Windows computers being sold, there will soon be an awful lot of Internet Explorer users out there on the Internet.

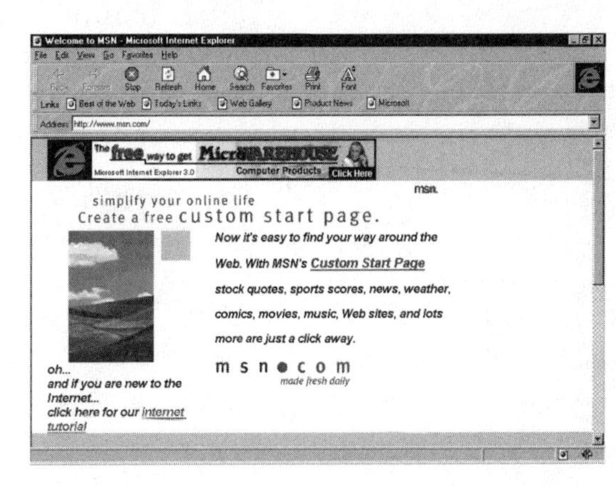

Inevitably, Microsoft have their own set of extensions to vanilla HTML. Some of them can be simply annoying (the way you can play a tune when you open a page is a case in point), but some of them, such as style sheets, can be very useful for sophisticated web design.

When you are designing a web page, you should bear in mind that not everyone will be using your favourite browser, and the page should still be at least partly meaningful for them. Remember also, that not everyone will be using the latest version of the relevant software, and that not all features are available on all versions of a browser. The Windows 3.1 version of a browser will generally not have all the features of the Windows 95/ Windows NT version, and the Mac version will be different again.

HTML, HEAD and BODY tags

Officially, all the text of an HTML document should be contained between an <HTML> tag and a </HTML> tag. These are to identify the document as being in HTML, rather than in some other type of SGML. In reality, most browsers don't particularly care about these tags and a lot of people leave them out; but we want to do things *correctly,* right?

The <HEAD> section

Within the <HTML> tags, the next element is the document head. Every HTML document should have a head, but in practice again you can get away without one in some circumstances. The Head section comes between a <HEAD> and a </HEAD> tag.

```
<HTML>
<HEAD>
<TITLE>Title of the document</TITLE>
</HEAD>
<BODY>
...
Body of the document
</BODY>
</HTML>
```

The Head section contains information about the document as a whole. There are some special tags which should be used in the Head section:

<TITLE>

Text between a <TITLE> and a </TITLE> tag is supplied to the browser as the title of the document. Most browsers display this at the top of the window, and also use the title of the document in Bookmark and history lists. For full conformance, every HTML document should have a title definition.

Because the title of a page may turn up in a bookmark list weeks after someone has visited it, choose something which will identify your document globally – that is, in terms of the whole Internet. A title like "Introduction" will mean nothing if someone finds it in their bookmark list; "Such-and-such web page: Introduction" will be clearer.

The meanings of the terms relative and fully qualified addresses are explained on page 47.

<BASE>

When you are writing your web page, it is a good idea to specify the location of images and links using relative addresses, rather than fully qualified addresses. This is fine normally, but it means that if someone takes a copy of your HTML document for local use, then the links won't work. You can solve this by putting a BASE tag in the head section of the document.

A BASE tag should have one attribute, called "HREF" (that's short for "HyperText Reference": we'll see it a lot when we come to anchor tags). The value of the HREF attribute *must* be an absolute URL. The browser will put this URL on the beginning of every relative URL in the document.

There are a couple of other tags allowed in the HEAD section, but they have pretty esoteric uses, so these will be described as and when we need them.

You should never put text in the Head section – it won't be displayed.

The <BODY> section

The bulk of an HTML document is found in the Body section. A few sorts of HTML document do not have a Body section – if you're using frames, for example – but most do. The Body section begins with a "<BODY>" tag, and ends with a "</BODY>" tag.

The BODY tag can have a number of attributes which allow you to specify a background image or background and foreground colours. These attributes were originally Netscape extensions to HTML, though they have now been included in HTML 3.2. Most browsers can now handle them, but you will find the odd one which can't. Be very careful about your choices of colours – it's very easy to make your page totally unreadable this way (especially, remember that not everyone has the same number of colours on their machine as you do). The attributes are as follows:

BACKGROUND

The BACKGROUND attribute specifies an image file (usually a .GIF file), which will be used as the background. Its value should be the URL of the file. The file will be repeated as necessary to fill the background (rather like a windows wallpaper file). It's important to make an image file as small as possible, because if you use a large file as a background your page will appear to be *very* slow to download.

BGCOLOR

HTML was written by Americans – so don't try to spell "color" with a "u".

This attribute specifies the colour to use for the background. This can be specified in one of two ways, one easy, one more complicated. The simpler way is to use one of the permitted colour names: aqua, black, blue, fuchsia, gray, green, lime, maroon, navy, olive, purple, red, silver, teal, white or yellow. If you want more control, you should specify the colour in what's called "RGB" notation. This is covered on the following two pages.

TEXT

This attribute defines the colour you want your text.

LINK

This defines the colour in which to display HyperText links which have not yet been visited.

VLINK

This defines the colour for links which have previously been visited.

ALINK

This defines the colour of the link as you actually click it with the mouse.

Describing colours in RGB notation

"RGB" stands for "Red-Green-Blue", and refers to the way that your computer handles colours.

Computers produce a colour display by combining the three additive primary colours – red, green and blue – in proportions. So a bright red would be 100% red and 0% blue and green. White is 100% of red, blue and green. Pale green would be 100% green, 90% red and blue – oh, and black is 0% of all three. Computers store colours as a series of three numbers – one for red, one for blue and one for green. To make things even more complicated, the numbers are written in hexadecimal notation – that's "base 16" if you remember your GCSE Maths.

In normal ("base 10") counting, 10 means "one ten, and 0 units" (it's all coming back, isn't it?). In hexadecimal, "10" means "one 16 and 0 units" – that's sixteen in real money. I see what you're asking: "so what do we do when we've got an eleven?" I hear you ask (I do hear you ask, don't I?). Well, hexadecimal works like this:

Decimal		Hexadecimal	
1	=	1	
2	=	2	
3	=	3	
4	=	4	
5	=	5	
6	=	6	
7	=	7	
8	=	8	
9	=	9	(pretty dull so far, huh?)
10	=	A	(Uh-oh...)
11	=	B	
12	=	C	
13	=	D	
14	=	E	
15	=	F	

Just to make it more confusing, you can recognise a hexadecimal number because it has a "#" in front of it. So, "#FF" in English is "255" (work it out...), and "#00" is... zero. Getting back to our subject, #FFFFFF is hexadecimal RGB for white and #000000 is hex RGB for black. #FF0000 is a really strong red, #00FF00 is a really strong green and... well, you can work it out. If you search really hard there are RGB colour charts available on the Net.

RGB notation gives each colour a range between 0 and 255. In binary notation, this takes up 8 bits (binary digits). With eight bits for each of the three binary colours, that makes 24 bits of colour information. A "24 bit" display card is able to display this many colours all at once – but let's face it, not everyone has a 24 bit display card. Most lesser cards can choose from a palette of this many colours, but can only display a limited number of them – an 8 bit card can only display 256 at a time. Old VGA adapters can only display 16 colours at once, and have a much more limited palette. This is important to remember when choosing colours, because if the display can't produce the colour you ask for, it will do the best it can to choose one near to it. This, unfortunately, often totally destroys your carefully-chosen colour scheme.

In general, when choosing colours for a web page, you're fairly safe if you assume that most people on the Internet have a machine which can display 256 colours. Images will take up some of these values, though. The safest route is to choose from only five hexadecimal values for your colours: 00, 40, 80, c0 and ff. This gives you a choice of 125 possible colours and most machines will be able to handle them.

Headings

Headings divide your body text into sections. There are six types of headings in the HTML specification. H1 is the most important, then come H2, H3 and so on down to H6, which is the least important.

One thing you should remember is that the HTML standard does *not* specify the actual appearance of any particular heading style – that's up to the browser, and in some browsers the user can apply their specifications for how a particular style is rendered. In particular, it's poor style to use a header style to produce bolder or more prominent text – it will usually work, but you can never guarantee it, and that's not what headers are for.

REMEMBER

The browser will separate a header from the text around it automatically – you don't have to put in extra space yourself.

In practice it's difficult to keep to it, but in theory you should try and go up and down heading styles one at a time: so a 1-Heading would contain a few 2-Headings, each of which would contain a couple of 3-Headings, which in turn contains 4-Headings, and so on. Headings look like this:

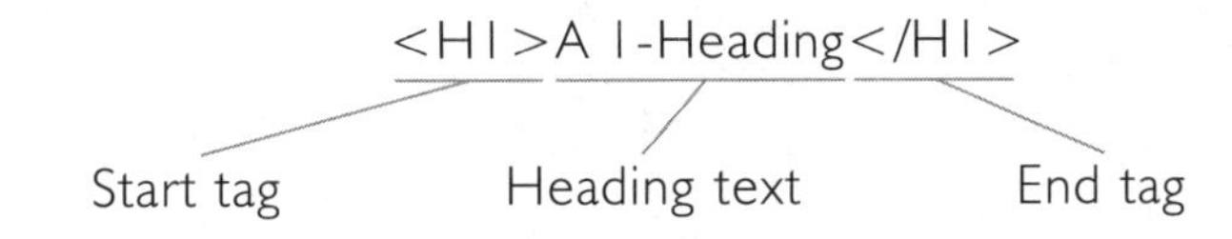

Your start and end tags must agree: so if the start tag is <H1> and the end tag is </H2> your code will go wrong. This is a surprisingly easy mistake to make, so be careful.

Marquee text

This only currently works with Internet Explorer.

One very effective way of creating eye-catching text is to use the MARQUEE tag. This scrolls text across the page, just like the "Scrolling Marquee" screensaver that is shipped with Windows. To do this, simply place some text between a <MARQUEE> and a </MARQUEE> tag. There are many attributes that can be used with this tag, but you should be able to achieve good effects using many of the attributes you would apply to images, like ALIGN, WIDTH, HEIGHT, etc., to control the properties of the box through which the text scrolls.

Paragraphs

The <P> tag designates a paragraph. There is some confusion as to exactly how the paragraph tag should be used. One method is like this:

```
<P>This is a paragraph...
```

Notice that the <P> tag goes at the start of the paragraph. Another method treats the tag as a container:

```
<P>This is another paragraph. Note how it's contained within
start and end tags.</P>
```

The third method considers the <P> tag to make the *break* between paragraphs:

```
This is yet another paragraph.<P>
```

All three methods will work, though they produce subtly different effects. Use whichever style you're happy with.

The browser will lay out a paragraph as a continuous block of text. Any carriage returns or tabs that you place in the text will be ignored.

If you use the <P>-first method, some browsers will allow you to include an ALIGN attribute. <P ALIGN=LEFT> is the normal setup, where the paragraph is aligned to the left; ALIGN=RIGHT makes your paragraph right-aligned (*not* justified, right-aligned), and ALIGN=CENTER will centre the paragraph.

Line breaks

The <BR> tag forces a line break. In normal text, this just inserts a carriage return. If you use a BR with the CLEAR attribute, it forces a move down to clear floating images. <BR CLEAR=LEFT> moves past floating images to the left, CLEAR=RIGHT does the same with images to the right, and CLEAR=ALL moves clear of all floating images.

Font styles

These tags affect the way that text is displayed. All of them need both a start and an end tag, and affect the text within the two tags, like this: <B>Bold Text</B>. The tags must be nested – that is: <B>Bold <I>or</B> Italic</I> is wrong, though <B>Bold <I>or Italic</I></B> works.

The tags are as follows:

<B>	**Bold** text
<I>	*Italic* text ✓
<U>	Underlined text ✓
<TT>	Puts the text in a monospaced font (it stands for "Teletype")
<STRIKE>	Strikethrough text
<BIG>	Puts text in a bigger font
<SMALL>	Puts text in a smaller font
<SUB>	Subscripts the text (moves it down)
<SUP>	Superscripts the text (moves it up)

There is also a group of these tags which describe the effect required, and leave the exact rendering to the browser:

<EM>	Emphasised text, usually rendered italic
<STRONG>	Strong text, usually rendered bold
<DFN>	Used for the definitions
<CODE>	Used for extracts of program code
<SAMP>	Used for sample output from a program
<KBD>	Used for text typed by a user (on the keyboard)
<VAR>	Used for variables in program functions
<CITE>	Used for citations and references

Font sizes

The FONT tag allows you to change the size or colour of the current font. HTML defines seven font sizes: font size 1 is the smallest, 7 is the largest.

The FONT tag is a container – that is, you must have a </FONT> tag at the end of the section it effects. The tag has these attributes:

SIZE

This sets the new font size (obviously). There are two ways you can use this attribute. You can specify an absolute size for the font, <FONT SIZE=6> for example. Otherwise you can specify the font size relative to the current BASEFONT setting. See the section below for details of BASEFONT. A relative font size is expressed like this:

<FONT SIZE="+3"> or

<FONT SIZE="-2">

The actual font size can never be smaller than 1 or bigger than 7.

COLOR

This specifies the colour of the font. It has the same possible values as the BACKGROUND attribute of the BODY tag.

The BASEFONT tag

The BASEFONT tag defines the font size that relative font sizes are worked out from. There is no end tag – you just need a single tag. The tag has one attribute, SIZE which you have to include (because otherwise the tag wouldn't do anything at all).

If you don't have a BASEFONT tag, the basefont size for the document is considered to be 3.

Other layout tags

There are a number of other HTML tags which affect the way that text is laid out. All of these tags are containers – that is, they affect the text between the start and end tags.

<PRE> – preformatted text

Normally, a web browser will lay out the text in an HTML document so that it fits neatly in the browser's window. Any ends of lines, extra spaces, tabs etc. which you include will be replaced by a single space. Most of the time this is a good idea – as with a word processor, you don't need to worry where lines end. In some cases, for example if you are laying out a poem, you actually want the carriage returns left as you made them. In this case you should enclose the text in <PRE> tags.

Text in a PRE tag is displayed in a fixed font – that is, a font in which all letters are the same width, as against a proportionally-spaced font, where an "i" is much narrower than an "m". A fixed font makes it much easier to line up columns made up of spaces and such like.

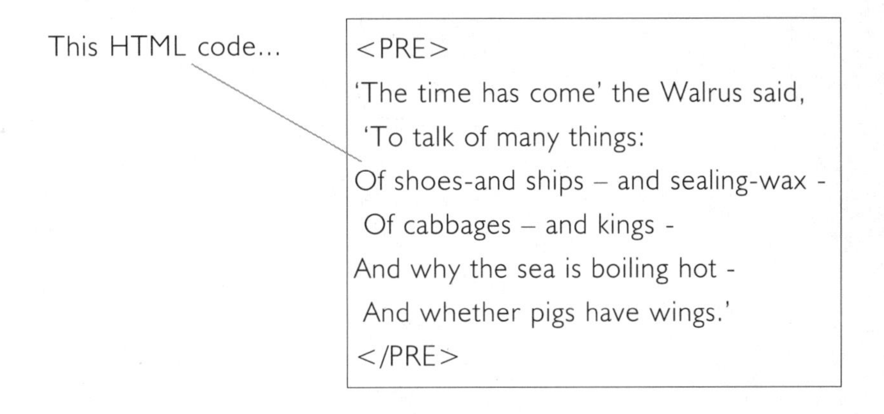


```
'The time has come' the Walrus said,
 'To talk of many things:
Of shoes-and ships - and sealing-wax -
 Of cabbages - and kings -
And why the sea is boiling hot -
 And whether pigs have wings.'
```

...will look like this in Netscape Navigator

Within a PRE tag you should be careful about which HTML tags you use. Those which change the size or appearance of the text (like FONT tags) will not work.

DIV and CENTER

HTML uses American spellings, so it's "CENTER", not "CENTRE".

The DIV Tag is part of HTML 3.0, so not all browsers will handle it. A DIV tag is used to designate a "division" of the text. The DIV tag has one attribute: ALIGN. Text within <DIV ALIGN=LEFT> will be left-aligned, like normal text. ALIGN=RIGHT will be aligned to the right margin, and ALIGN=CENTER will produce centred text.

The CENTER tag does exactly the same as <DIV ALIGN=CENTER>, and is an earlier bit of HTML which has been retained because it is so common on the web.

BLOCKQUOTE

Text contained within a BLOCKQUOTE tag is formatted as a separate paragraph, and most browsers display it indented.

ADDRESS

Text contained in an ADDRESS tag should contain information identifying the author of the page in question. Use an ADDRESS tag to put in your name, eMail address, home page location, even your (street) address if you're brave enough.

The ADDRESS tag is usually displayed in italic text. You can put other tags in an ADDRESS tag, like <EM> tags, or anchors to other pages etc.

Lists

HTML has a number of tags to describe different types of lists of things. All lists have the same basic syntax: the difference is the way they are displayed. You can have lists within lists: this is useful for tables of contents, and such like.

Unordered lists

The simplest type of list is an unordered list. The elements of an unordered list are usually displayed as a series of bullet points.

An unordered list is contained between <UL> and </UL> tags. Each element in the list should be started by an <LI> tag.

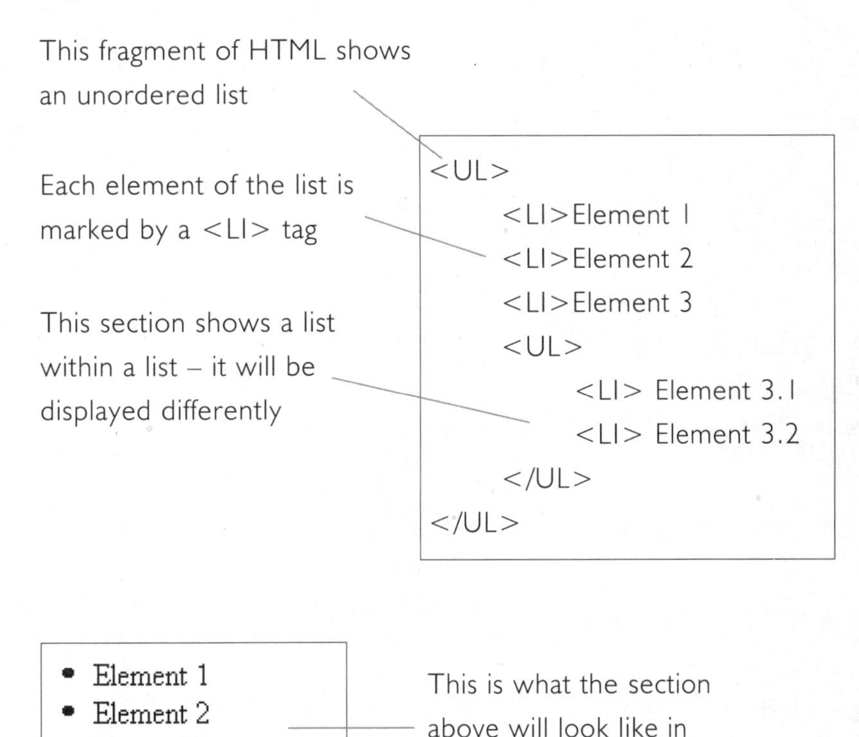

Ordered lists

An ordered list is just like an unordered list, but the elements are displayed numbered. The browser will work out the numbering scheme for you.

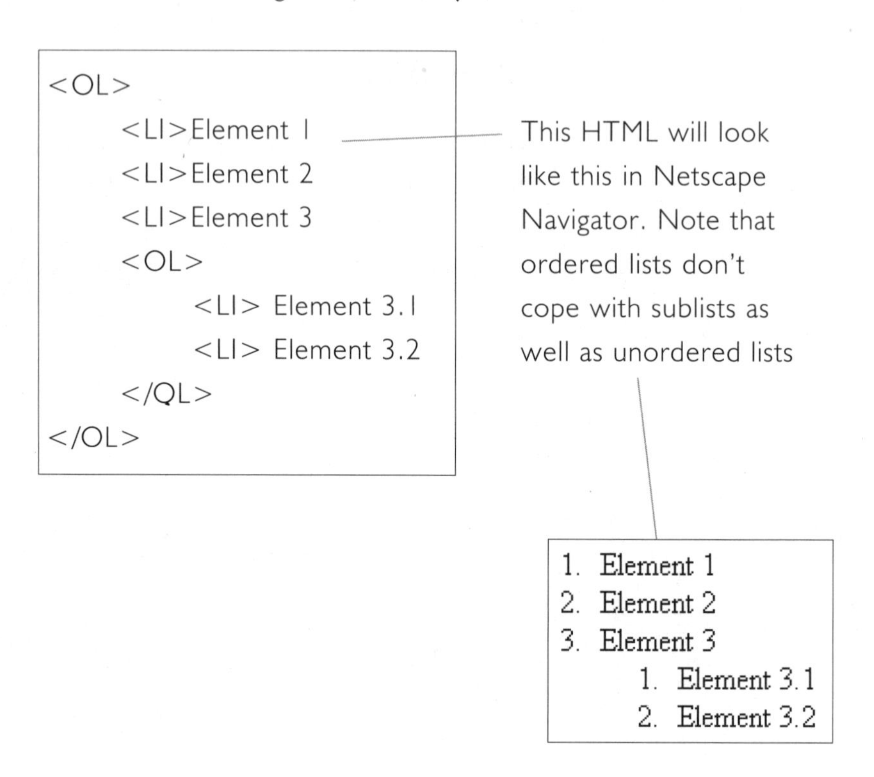

DIR and MENU

These two list styles are intended for directory listings and for menus of options respectively. They are supposed to be more compact than normal lists, but Netscape Navigator at least displays them just like a UL.

Hyperlinks

The important bit about HTML is of course the ability to put in HyperText links. This is done using the A (for "Anchor") tag.

An Anchor tag looks like this:

<A HREF=somewhere>The Anchor</A>

The "HyperText Reference" attribute defines the URL of the destination of the anchor

The section between the <A> and the </A> is the body of the anchor: this is the bit which will be underlined by the browser

In general, you can put anything you like in the body of the anchor. One trick is to put an <IMG> anchor there: that will make the image into a button.

The Anchor tag has the following attributes:

HREF

You'll sometimes see someone talking about a "fully qualified" URL. This just means the complete URL.

The value of this attribute gives the location which the link points to. Normally, this is the URL of the page which you wish to go to when the anchor is clicked on. If the page is on the same server, then you don't have to write in the complete URL of the page. This is called a "relative" URL, and in this case the base address of the current page (the site name and directory) is added on to the filename you provide. It's often a good idea to use relative URLs, because it means that it doesn't matter where exactly the pages are finally placed, they will still work. However, if you always use full URLs, then someone can save your page to their local disk, and it will still work OK.

You can point an anchor to a place other than the top of a file. If you specify "HREF=somefile.htm#somewhere", the browser will fetch the file "somefile.htm", and display it so that the anchor named "somewhere" is at the top of the window. If you use "HREF=#somwhereelse" the browser will go to the anchor named "somewhereelse" in the current document.

REMEMBER

HTML files should end with ".html"; however, DOS only allows 3-character file extensions, so you can use ".htm" too.

The HREF of an anchor doesn't have to be another HTML file (though it often is). You can point an anchor at any sort of file, as long as it's on the server. If the file is not HTML, the browser will download it. What it does with the file when it's got it depends on the type of the file – and more particularly, on its type designation (the bit of the file name after the "."). A file which ends with ".html" or ".htm" will be assumed to be HTML, and the browser will try to display it, even if it isn't really HTML (it's hard to see why you would have another type of file ending in .htm, but you never know). A text file (ending in ".txt") will be displayed as plain text by the browser. A GIF or JPEG image will usually be displayed on its own by the browser. This can be useful if you've got a big image file that you want people to be able to get at, but you want the page to download quickly: make a small "thumbnail" of the image, and make it an anchor to the full-screen version.

What happens to other types of files depends on whether the browser has a "helper application" defined for the particular type. If there is a helper defined, then that application is run; if not, the file is saved to hard disk. This makes it easy to make archives of software etc. available on the web.

TITLE

If you specify a TITLE attribute, this text is displayed on the bottom line of the browser if you point to the anchor with the mouse, but don't click on it.

NAME

If you specify a NAME attribute, then that anchor can be specified as the destination of another anchor. For example, if you put <A NAME=index> into a document, then you can point to that part of your document like this: <A HREF=#index>. A named anchor can itself point to somewhere else (that is, it also has an HREF attribute), or you can stop it from showing up on a page by immediately following it by a </A> tag, like this:

```
<A NAME=end></A>
```

Horizontal rules

The <HR> tag ends a paragraph, and inserts a horizontal line across the screen. It has the following attributes:

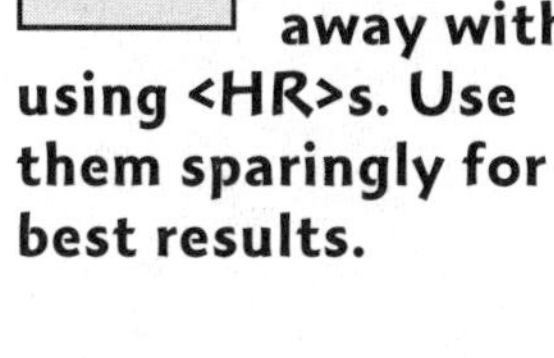

It's very easy to get carried away with using <HR>s. Use them sparingly for best results.

ALIGN

The ALIGN attribute can have the value of LEFT, RIGHT or CENTER. It gives the vertical alignment of the rule. Note that unless the WIDTH attribute is changed, this has no effect.

NOSHADE

Normally, the line of an HR is shaded, so that it looks like this: . If you do <HR NOSHADE>, it comes out looking like this:

SIZE

This attribute describes the thickness of the line, in pixels.

WIDTH

The WIDTH attribute tells the browser how long the line of an HR should be. You can express it in two ways. If you use <HR WIDTH=75>, it tells the browser that the line should be 75 pixels long (regardless of how wide the screen is). On the other hand, <HR WIDTH="75%"> will make the line 75% of the current width of the screen.

Basic HTML – an example

Many of the concepts covered in this chapter are applied in the example below, which uses a simplified version of a page from Computer Step's web site. Compare the screenshot with the HTML code that follows.

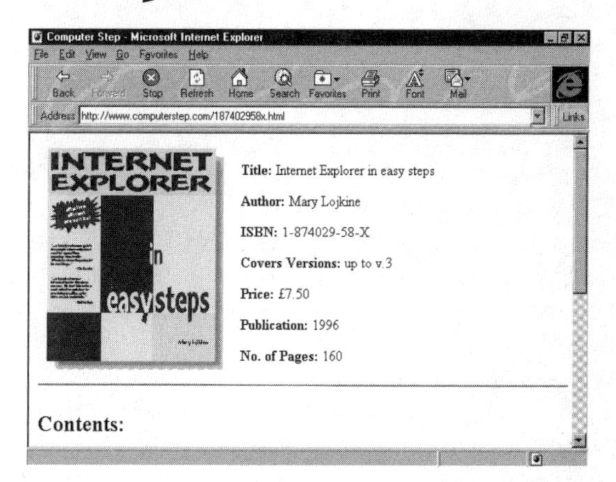

<html> <head><title>Computer Step</title></head>	*Opens the HTML document*
<body bgcolor="#ffffff">	*Sets background colour to white*
<img src="187402958x.gif" align="left" hspace="10">	*Places image, aligned left*
 	Line break
<b>Title:</b> Internet Explorer in easy steps<p> <b>Author:</b> Mary Lojkine<p> <b>ISBN:</b> 1-874029-58-X<p> <b>Covers Versions:</b> up to v.3<p> <b>Price:</b> £7.50<p> <b>Publication:</b> 1996<p> <b>No. of Pages:</b> 160	*Displays text, with headings in bold, and with a paragraph break at the end of each line*
<br clear=left>	*"Clear" line break makes what follows appear below image*
<hr size=2 align=center width=100% noshade>	*Horizontal line*
 <h2 align="left">Contents:</h2>	*"Contents" heading*
1. Getting Started 13. Newsgroups Index	*Lists contents (most entries have been omitted, to save space)*
<hr size=2 align=center width=100% noshade>	*Horizontal line*
</body> </html>	*Closes body and HTML*

Certain aspects of this web page would be presented better if we were to organise the information here using methods that have not yet been covered. In particular, the graphics and text could be aligned more effectively by using a table. Chapter Six covers the use of tables to hold text and other objects.

CHAPTER FOUR

Images

This chapter explains about using images in web pages, and gives you tips on how to get the best results.

Covers

The <IMG> tag

You place images into an HTML file using the IMG tag. The IMG tag doesn't have an end tag, but it does have a number of allowable attributes.

SRC

The SRC attribute defines the name of the file in which the image is to be found. Normally it is just the filename, but you can put in a complete URL – so you could get an image from anywhere on the Internet, if you really wanted to. It's not usually a good idea to use images on a remote site – first the site may not always be available, in which case your page may not display properly; second, and more importantly, the other site may change and your image may change or go away completely, in which case your page won't work any more!

```
This is a picture of me
<IMG SRC="andy.gif">
```

This code in an HTML file...

...will look like this using Netscape Navigator

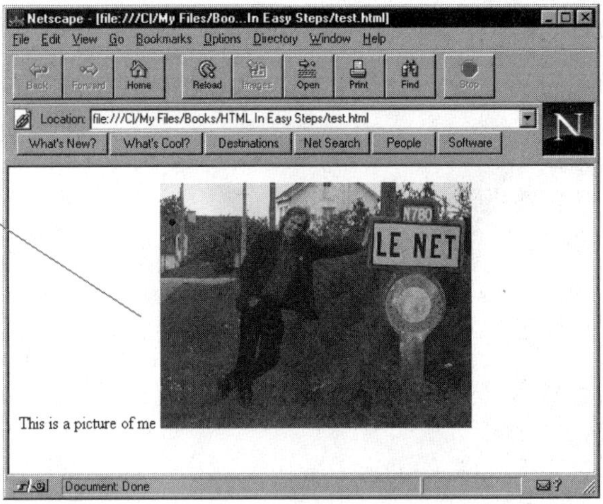

ALT

The value of the ALT attribute should be some text describing the image. There are a number of reasons to do this. Firstly, this message is displayed where the image will go until the image is downloaded, so your page makes sense as soon as possible. Secondly, not everyone has image downloading set up, either because their Internet connection is slow or because their browser doesn't display images (there are browsers like this, even nowadays). If you didn't have an ALT tag your page will make no sense to these people.

HEIGHT, WIDTH

These two attributes specify the height and width the browser will reserve for the image, in pixels. If you specify these attributes when naming the source file for the image, then the layout won't change when the image appears. It looks a lot neater that way.

Each little square of colour on your screen is called a pixel. It's short for "picture element".

If your image isn't the size that you specify for the HEIGHT and WIDTH attributes, the browser will rescale the image.

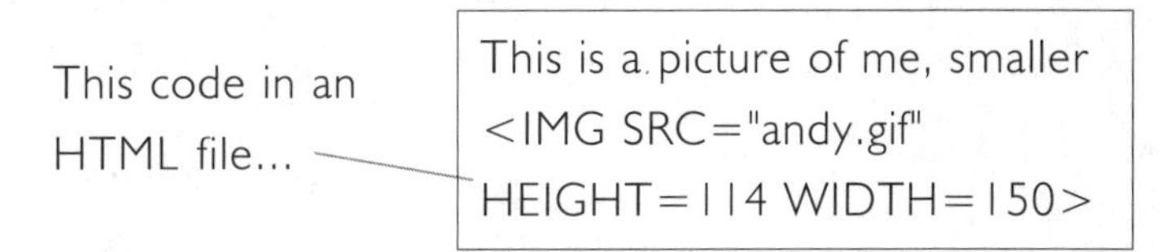

Only scale images by an exact multiple of their real size, otherwise they usually look horrid.

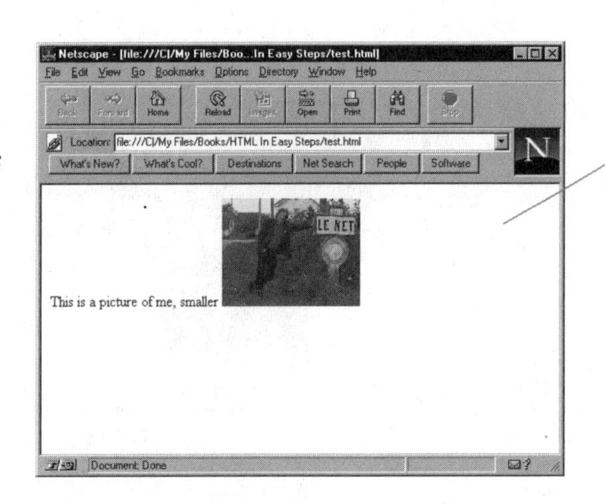

...will look like this using Netscape Navigator

ALIGN

This attribute describes how the image should be aligned with respect to the surrounding space. There are a number of different settings for this, and it's easiest if we go through these one at a time:

ALIGN=TOP

This means that the top of the image should align with the top of the highest element of the line on which it appears.

This is what ALIGN=TOP looks like. See how the image aligns with the top of the text

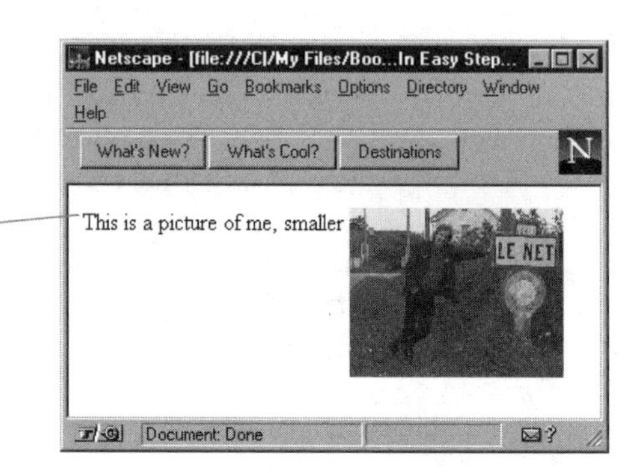

ALIGN=BOTTOM

This means the bottom of the image aligns with the bottom of the line of text. This is the effect if you don't specify an ALIGN attribute.

ALIGN=CENTER

This means that the image is centred with respect to the text next to it.

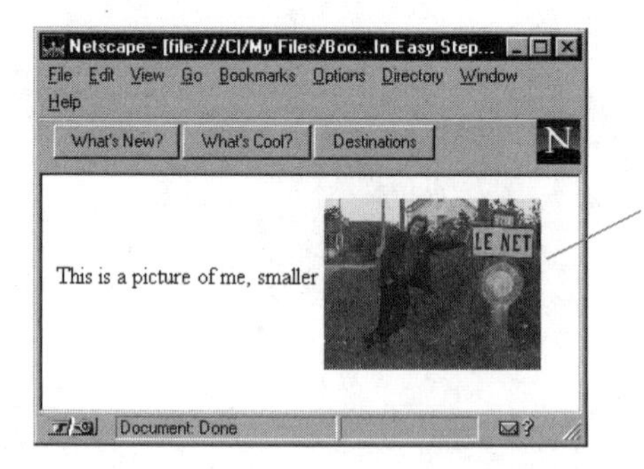

This is the effect of ALIGN=CENTER. See how the centre line of the text aligns with the vertical centre of the image

The last three settings only affect the line of text the image appears on. The next line of text will appear below the image. To do proper text wrapping (as used in this book) use these settings:

ALIGN=LEFT
The image is placed against the left margin, and text wraps to its right.

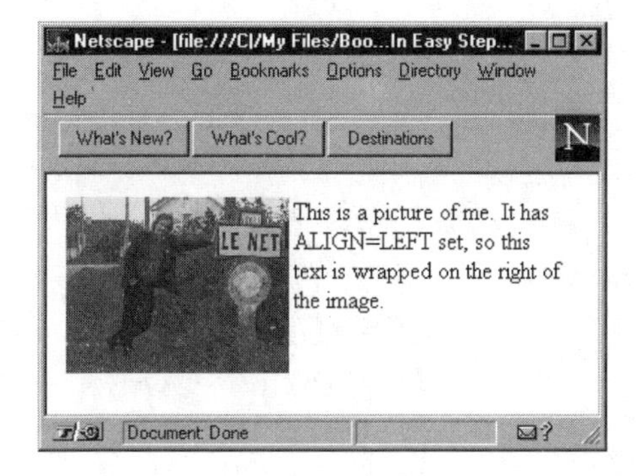

ALIGN=RIGHT
The image is placed against the right margin, and text is wrapped to the left of it.

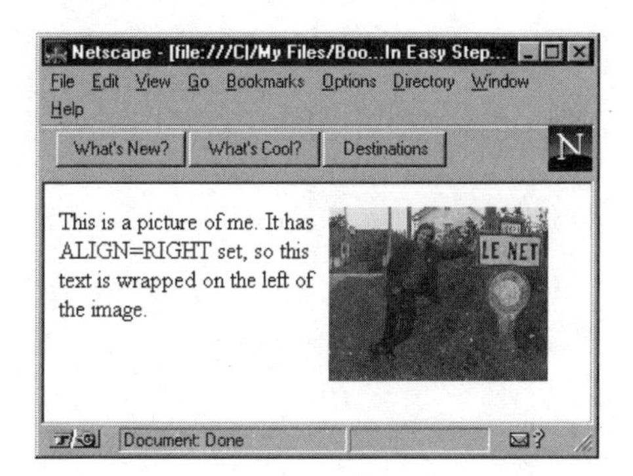

ISMAP

This tells the browser that this image is an Image Map. See Chapter Five to find out how to set these up.

BORDER

This specifies the width in pixels of the border around the image. In particular, if you specify BORDER=0 then an image which is a hyperlink will not have a coloured line around it.

HSPACE, VSPACE

The HSPACE attribute specifies how much blank space, in pixels, the browser should put to the left and right of the image. VSPACE specifies the amount of space to put above and below the image.

LOWSRC (Netscape Navigator only)

This attribute, which is not recognised by Internet Explorer, is designed to speed up the process of browsing web pages, particularly when those pages contain large images that may take a long time to download. LOWSRC is a companion to the SRC attribute, and takes the same argument (i.e., the URL of an image to be placed on the page). The only difference is that LOWSRC is intended to refer to a lower-resolution image which gives a taste of what the detailed image will look like; this is loaded first. If the user decides that they want to view the detailed image, it will be loaded automatically once the rest of the page's contents have been loaded. If they don't wish to see it, they can promptly link to another page.

LOWSRC should be included within the IMG tag, along with its companion SRC attribute, e.g.:

```
<IMG LOWSRC="lowres.gif" SRC="highres.gif">
```

If no SRC attribute exists, then not even the LOWSRC image will be displayed. Using the LOWSRC attribute will not confuse Internet Explorer or other browsers; they will simply ignore it, and display the SRC image.

Image formats

World-Wide Web browsers can handle a range of different image file formats, but today two formats are the most common: GIF and JPEG.

The GIF format was invented (and is owned) by CompuServe, the on-line service providers. Like the windows .BMP format, it stores the image as a rectangular grid of pixels, specifying the colour of each pixel in the image. A GIF file is much smaller than the equivalent BMP file because it uses special compression to group together patches of continuous colour. GIF files are good for drawn graphics and text, because they produce a small file and bold, clear lines. They can only have a maximum of 256 colours, so photographs don't come out as well. You can produce a GIF file with a transparent background, which looks nice if your page has a background image.

If you find that your GIF files are too large, consider using the new PNG format. GIF files perform compression by analysing horizontal bands of the same colour; PNG files, on the other hand, can analyse both horizontal and vertical areas. Consequently, they can achieve compression levels up to 30% better than GIFs.

GIF files can also contain a series of images: recent web browsers can use these to produce moving images. This is very useful, and will be covered later in this chapter.

The JPEG format was produced by an Internet committee called the "Joint Photographic Expert Group" – thus the name J-P-E-G. JPEG images use special psychological methods in their encoding. Fine detail is lost, but for photographs it produces a better-looking image than a GIF file will. When you produce a JPEG image you can specify how faithfully you want the image to be replaced: with a low accuracy level you can get amazing compression levels – it's possible to produce quite acceptable images which are under 1K in length. JPEG images don't work well if there is text or solid patches of colour in the image – the boundary comes out fuzzy.

GIF files

There are a number of different versions of the .GIF format, describing when the version was defined. Software which can handle a particular version of the format can always handle older versions of the format.

The oldest version of the format is called GIF87a. This is the "basic" version of the format. The more advanced version is called GIF89a. This extension allows you to specify one colour in the GIF to be transparent, to attach comments to a file, to produce multi-image ("animated") files, and to produce an image in what's referred to as "interlaced" format.

Interlaced GIF files

A normal GIF file specifies the image one line at a time, starting at the top of the image and working downwards. An interlaced GIF also specifies one line at a time, but puts the lines in a different order in the file, so that the whole image has at least *some* information from the beginning.

This is a non-interlaced .GIF file part-way through downloading over the Internet. The image has only got this far

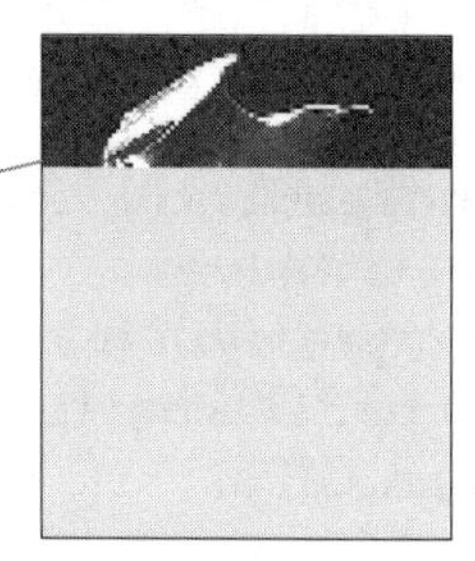

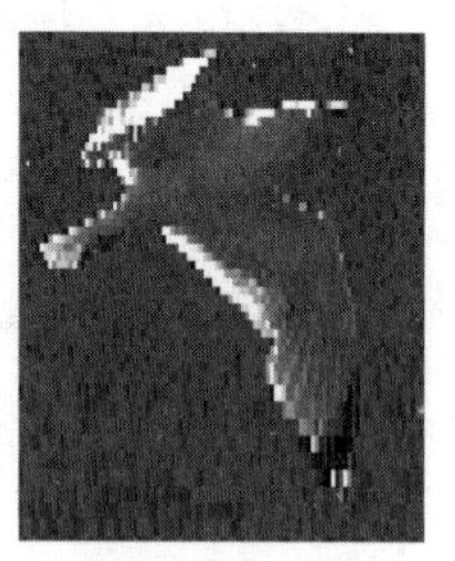

This is the same image, also part-way through loading, but this time the image is interlaced. Already we know what the image looks like

The effect of this becomes clear when you are downloading the image over the Internet. A non-interlaced GIF fills from the top down, as you would expect. An interlaced GIF appears initially out of focus – a bit like those bits on Crimewatch where they're disguising someone's face – and the image then gradually comes into focus. This means that someone looking at your page will get the general idea of what the images are before they've been completely downloaded.

Transparent GIF Images

It is possible to specify one colour of a GIF89a image to be "transparent". Navigator will allow the background colour or pattern to show through. This allows you to put images on your page which are not just rectangular. Note that the transparent background is still part of the image, so you can't overlap images and if the image is a HyperText anchor, then the corners of the image are still a link.

Multiple-Image GIFs

The GIF89a standard allows for a single file to contain more than one image. For years nothing was done with this feature, but Netscape (followed by the others) used this format to produce animated images. It is possible to specify the amount of time between displaying successive frames, and also whether the animation loops when it gets to the end.

Animated GIFs can be very effective, but when they first appeared animated logos started popping up all over the place. The fashion may begin to get stale very soon, so you should only use an animated GIF if it's absolutely necessary.

At the worst, a ten-frame animated GIF will be ten times the size of a one-frame image. However, the format is clever enough to only encode the *differences* between successive frames, so if you're crafty you can get an effective animation in not much more space than the plain image.

JPEG images

The JPEG format was designed to render photographs, and other images intended to look realistic to humans. It uses various psychological tricks to suggest detail which is not actually there: the savings from this process can result in very small images indeed.

When you convert a file to JPEG format, most applications will ask for an "accuracy" value (some describe this as a "compression ratio"). If you choose a high accuracy, then you will retain all the detail in your image, but the resulting file will be very big – were you to choose 100% accuracy the image would be identical to an equivalent TIFF file, and would be just as big. If you are willing to go for a low accuracy, you can get a very small image size (images less than 100 bytes in size are possible), but you lose detail until eventually the image is almost unrecognisable.

Losing detail from an image doesn't sound like a very good idea, but for photographs it often doesn't matter – some people even say that a photo or a painting looks nicer on a lower accuracy setting since you are less aware of the pixels of the screen.

This is a copy of andy.gif which was copied off Photo-CD and saved as a JPEG at 75% accuracy. The file is 4,938 bytes long

This is the same picture, but saved at 25% accuracy. Note that some fine detail is lost (look at the sign). The file is 2,313 bytes long. As a comparison, the same image as a GIF file is 16,823 bytes long

JPEG has another advantage over GIF as a format, which is appropriate to its purpose as a format for displaying photographs. A GIF file can only have a maximum of 256 colours, which is fine for line art, but can make a photo look like a painting-by-numbers picture. All JPEG files are saved off in 24-bit format, allowing 16 million colours. Of course, unless you have a 24-bit graphics card, your PC can't display all of them at once, but reducing the number of colours at the graphics-card stage will produce a more realistic image. And, of course, those of your readers who do have 24-bit colours will see your pictures in all their glory.

There is a recent development on JPEG, called "progressive JPEG". In practice this has the same effect as interleaved GIF files. There are not many graphics packages which will generate progressive JPEGs, but if your package can handle them, then it's worth saving your images in this format.

There is an extension of JPEG called MPEG. This defines a standard for encoding video compactly. It is only one of a number of video formats that you will encounter on the Internet – there are a number of proprietary systems as well. The relevant thing here is that in an MPEG video, each frame is stored as a JPEG image.

How to get images

One problem to address is how to get your images into a form which computers can handle. Images produced using a computer art package are already machine-readable, and just need to be converted into .GIF or .JPEG format. Other types of artwork, such as photographs, are more difficult.

If you've got the negatives for the pictures you want to use, one excellent method of capturing images is to put the pictures onto Kodak Photo-CD. Any photo developing outlet can do this for you. They send your negatives off to Kodak, and about a week later you get a CD with your pictures on it. It costs about £5.00 for the blank CD, and 20p-50p per picture (it costs less if you put a whole film on). The CD will hold about 100 pictures, and you can take the CD back to put more on later. The nice bit is that Kodak do the scanning for you, so there's no messing around with getting a good scan. Each image is stored in a range of resolutions. Just put the CD in your CD-ROM drive, and use suitable software to convert the scans into GIF or JPEG.

Other methods of image capture mean extra hardware. One approach is to use a scanner. For pictures you really need a flat-bed scanner – the roller type don't usually provide sufficient quality. Expect to pay at least £400 for a good flat-bed scanner.

Another option to consider would be a digital camera. These start at about £250, and look like a normal compact camera except there's no film – you plug them into your computer and transfer the images onto hard disk. The images are only really good enough for a web page, but if you're going to take lots of pictures for computer use, then it's an option to consider.

Tips for good images

Image resolution

When you acquire your images, it's worth paying attention to the resolution in which they will eventually be displayed. Computer screens vary, but most of them have a resolution of about 72 dots per inch (dpi). Most scanners acquire images at 300-1200 dpi. If you put a 300 dpi image in a web page it will come out about four times its original size, which may not be what you were after.

If you change an image's resolution, always make sure you change it by an exact multiple – halve it or quarter it. If the factor by which you change the resolution is an odd amount the image will almost always come out looking awful. For an image scanned to 300 dpi, rescale it to be 75 dpi and accept that it will display a bit big – if you rescale it to 72 dpi the image will look awful.

Colour maps

Different PCs have different resolutions, but in general you can assume that most people who view your pages will have a screen capable of 256 colours at a time. Of this, Netscape Navigator takes about ten colours for its windows. If you can manage it, make sure that your images look OK viewed in this many colours. A surprising number of people have PCs with a VGA adapter, which can only handle 16 colours at once – a challenge, but worth bearing in mind.

A useful tip when working with GIF files is to try and keep the number of colours to a power of two. A sixteen-colour GIF can be saved as a four-bit GIF which is half the size of a 32-colour GIF (which needs to be saved in 5-bit format). In effect, this means that a 17-colour GIF is twice the size of a 16-colour one. The same effect applies with 2-colour, 4-colour, 8-colour, 64-colour and 128-colour images. If you can limit your icons to four or eight colours, you can benefit by generating very small files.

Building an animated GIF file

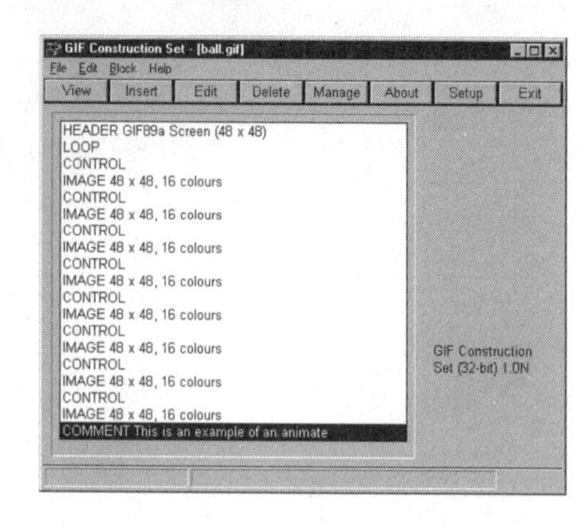

Producing an animated GIF file takes a while, but it is not difficult. There are a number of applications available to help you; an excellent one for Windows is GIF Construction Set, which is produced by a company called Alchemy Mindworks. The program is shareware, and you can download a copy from their web site:

http://www.mindworkshop.com

The steps to producing an animated GIF are as follows:

1. Produce the images which make up the frames of your image. Put each image in a separate file. GIF Construction Set can handle most image formats

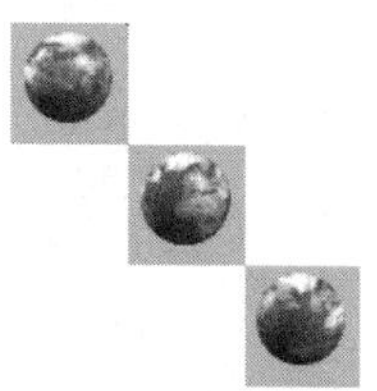

2. Select "Animation Wizard" from the File menu of GIF Construction Set

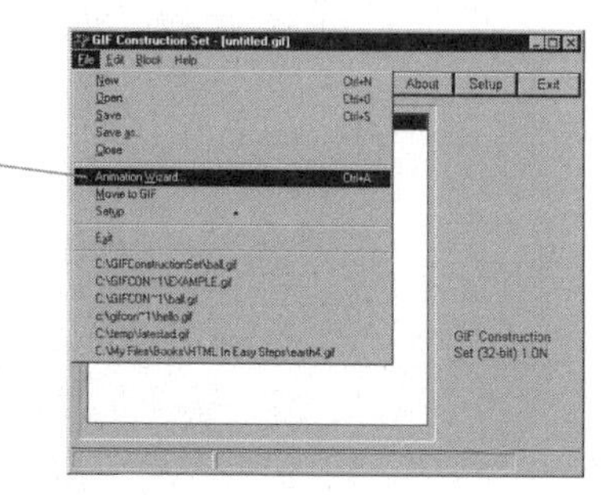

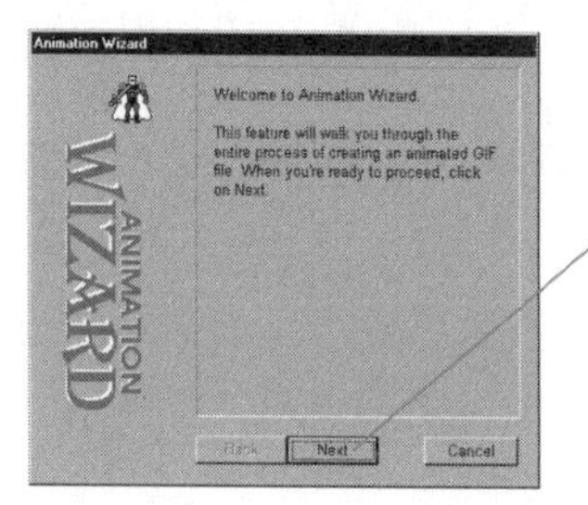

3. You will see the Animation Wizard dialogue box. Press "Next" to continue

4 The next dialogue box asks if your image is to be used on a web page. If you answer "yes", GIF Construction Set will use a palette of colours which match those used by Netscape Navigator

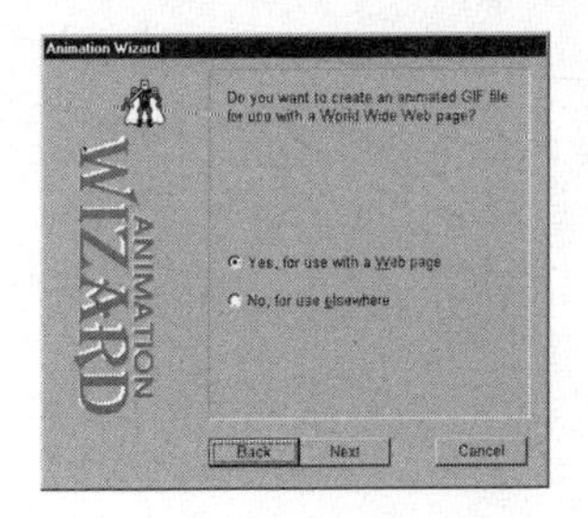

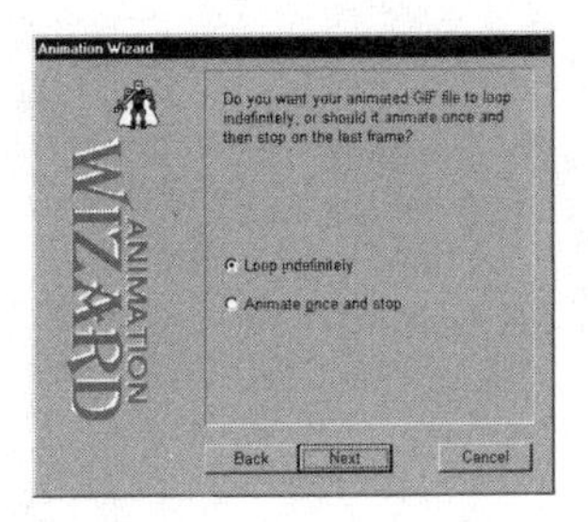

5 An animation can either run once and then stop, or it can loop endlessly. The next screen allows you to choose which

6 The next screen asks you whether the image is line art or scanned. Select the correct option, and press the "NEXT" button

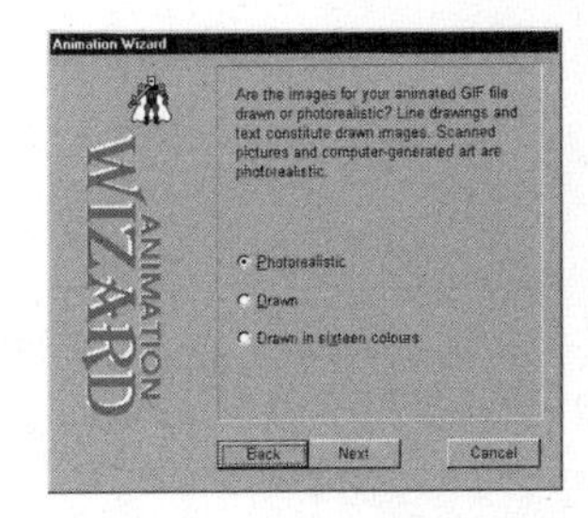

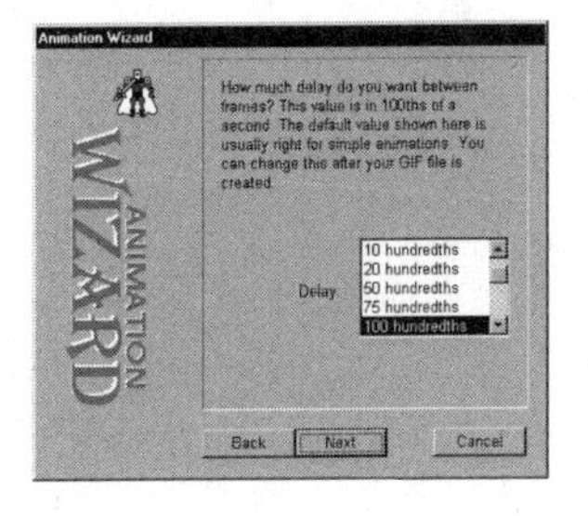

7 This screen lets you specify the delay between frames. You can change this after you've built the GIF file. It is even possible to have different delays between different frames

8 Now you are ready to select the images to make up your animation. Press this button to begin:

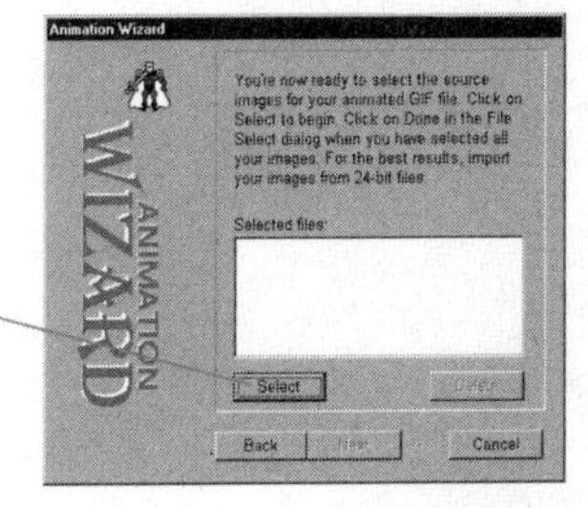

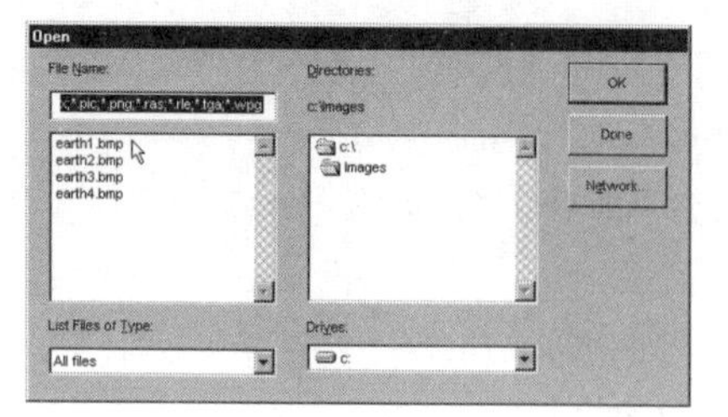

9 Select your files one at a time, in order. When you have finished, select the "Done" button

10 Now you have selected all the files, click on the "Next" button to generate your animated GIF

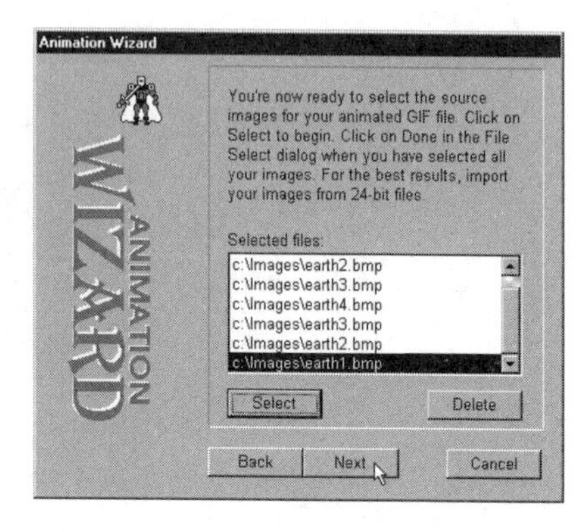

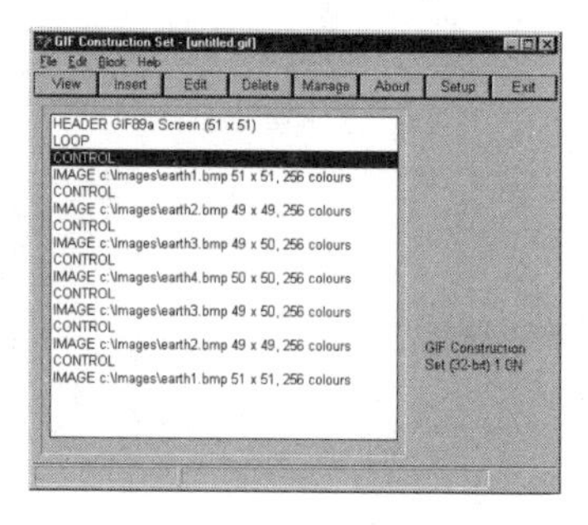

11 You can see the individual frames of the image in the main window. To edit any image or transition, just double-click it

CHAPTER FIVE

Image Maps

This chapter shows you how to use an image map to place hot areas on an image.

Covers

Client-side and server-side maps

There are two ways of implementing an image map. The older method is referred to as "server-side", and does the translation of the map coordinates into the URL using a CGI script on the server. Server-side image maps will work with any browser, but they're slower, because the server first has to do the translation, send the URL back to the browser, and the browser then has to request the URL.

The newer method is a Netscape innovation, so not all browsers can handle it. Client-side processing gets the browser to do the translation. This is faster from the user's point of view, since there's just a single fetch from the remote server.

It is possible to set up an image map so that those browsers which can handle it will use client-side, and the others will use server-side. This is the route which will be described in this chapter.

These "hidden" links are referred to as "Easter eggs".

There is one case in which you wouldn't want to use a client-side image map. It's possible to set up an image map as a puzzle – where the links are not immediately obvious, or where there are "hidden" links for those in the know. Client-side processing destroys this – as you move the mouse around over the image, the links appear on the bottom line of the browser just like a normal anchor.

Laying out an image map

A server-side image map is defined by its map file. This consists of a series of lines, one for each hot spot on the image map. Each line provides the following information:

- The shape of the hot spot;
- Coordinates defining the shape;
- The URL to which this hot spot points.

Hot spots can be rectangular, circular, oval or any arbitrary shape.

Check with your web space provider which format of map file to use, and then stick with it.

There are two different formats for the map file, which carry the same information arranged slightly differently. These are called the "NCSA" and the "CERN" formats, referring to the servers which handle them. All HTML servers handle one or the other format: some do both.

Client-side servers use a MAP tag which is placed in the HEAD region of the HTML file. This has an almost identical layout to a map file – and it's a simple process to edit a map file into an HTML document to produce a MAP tag.

It is possible to produce a map file by hand, but you don't really have to. A number of applications are available which will build your map file for you. Many HTML builder applications have a module to do this, and there are freeware stand-alone applications for this purpose. The following pages describe how to use "Map This", which is powerful, easy to use – and free. You can get Map This from its home page at:

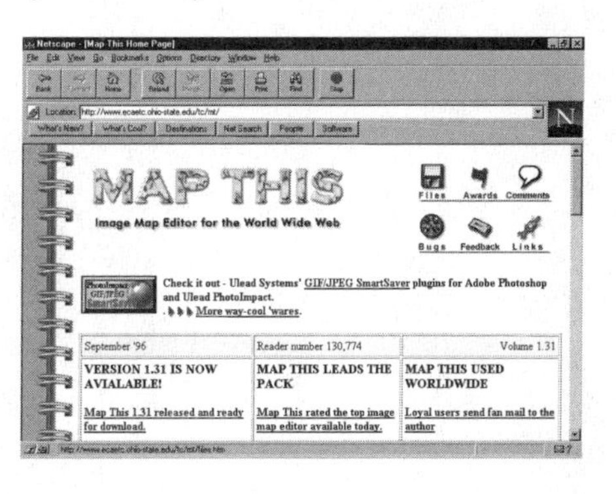

http://www.ecaetc.ohio-state.edu/tc/mt/

Building your image map

One common use of an image map is to have a map of an area, which the user can click to select areas. This can go to larger-scale maps and so on. For this example, we will use this map of the UK as our image. You can use anything for an image map – even a photograph.

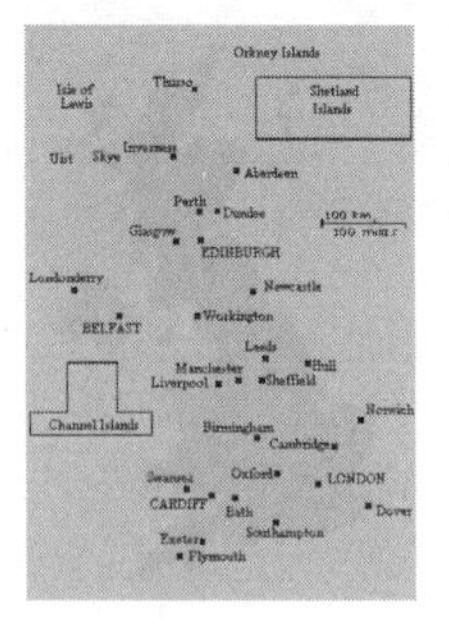

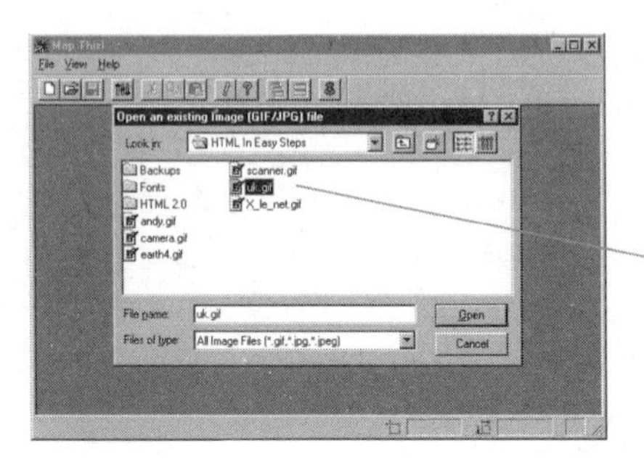

1 Select “New Map”. You will be asked for an image file. In this case, we choose “uk.gif”. Click “Open”

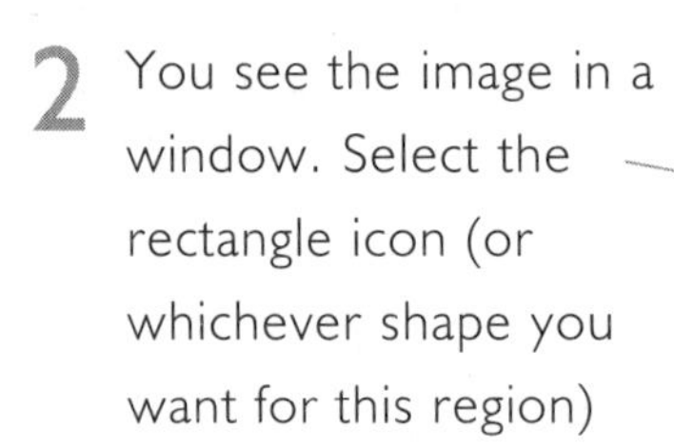

2 You see the image in a window. Select the rectangle icon (or whichever shape you want for this region)

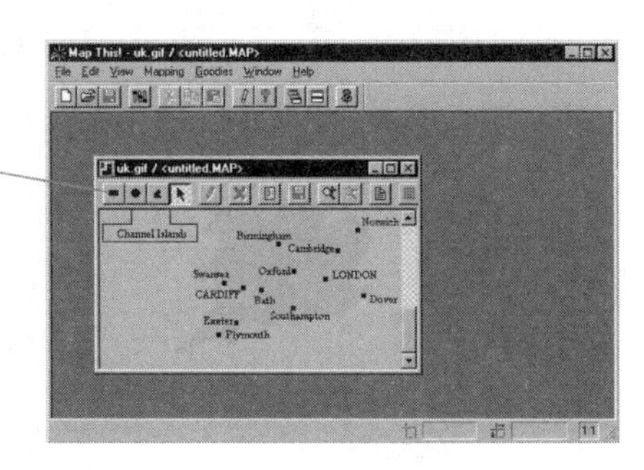

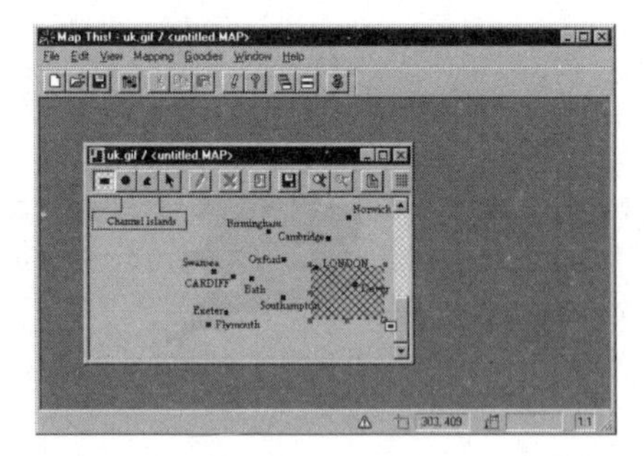

3 Click on the image and drag to make the region that you want (you can adjust the area afterwards)

Repeat this process for each hot area on your map. This is how to define an arbitrary polygon:

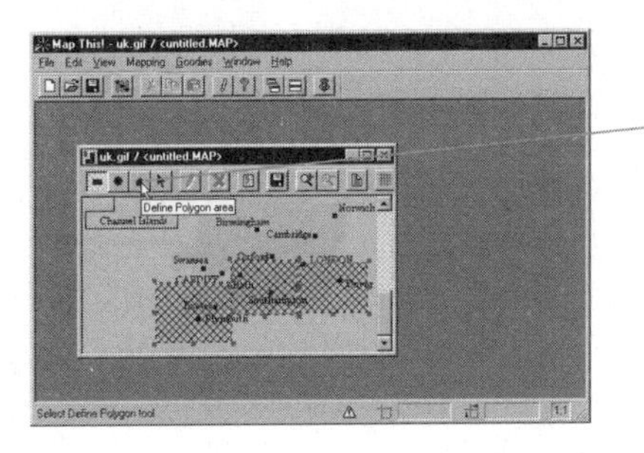

1 Click on the "polygon" button

2 Click at each corner of your polygon. Double-click to finish the polygon

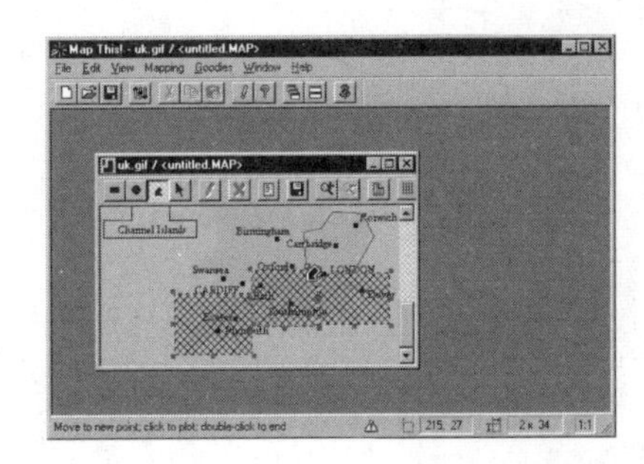

This is how to define where your hot spots point to:

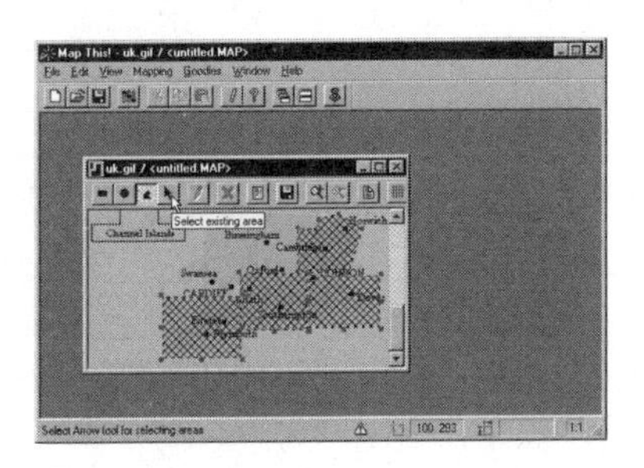

1 When you have finished defining your areas, select the pointer icon

2 Double-click on each hot area in turn

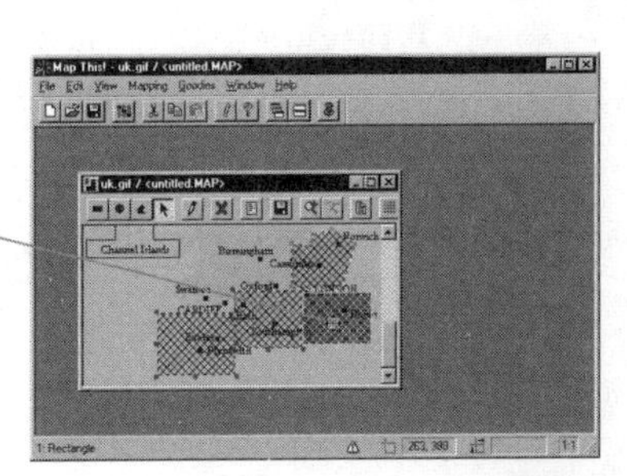

You will see this dialogue box:

3 Put the target URL in here

4 If you're using frames, you can put the frame name in here.

5 Put any comments here

When you're finished, choose "save". You will see this dialog:

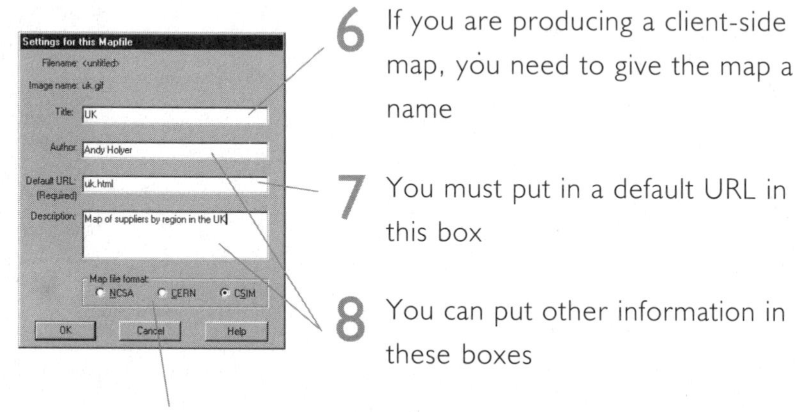

6 If you are producing a client-side map, you need to give the map a name

7 You must put in a default URL in this box

8 You can put other information in these boxes

9 Map This can produce maps for three formats: NCSA, CERN and CSIM (Client-Side Image Map). These buttons let you choose which to use

BEWARE **Map This places the MAP code at the end of the BODY section of an HTML file. It can also go in the HEAD section; it's easy to move it.**

If you are producing a server-side image map, you should save the file off as a .map file. If you are producing a client-side map, Map This will insert the MAP tag into an HTML file for you, so you can just choose an existing HTML file.

Making it work

Once you have produced your map file there is the matter of editing the HTML files to make it work. What you have to do depends on whether you are producing a client-side or a server-side image map. Remember that it is quite possible to set up both mechanisms: people who have a browser capable of handling client-side maps will have improved performance, and the others won't notice any difference.

Client-side maps

There are two components to a client-side image map:

- A MAP tag
- The IMG tag for the image itself

The MAP tag

The MAP tag will look a bit like this:

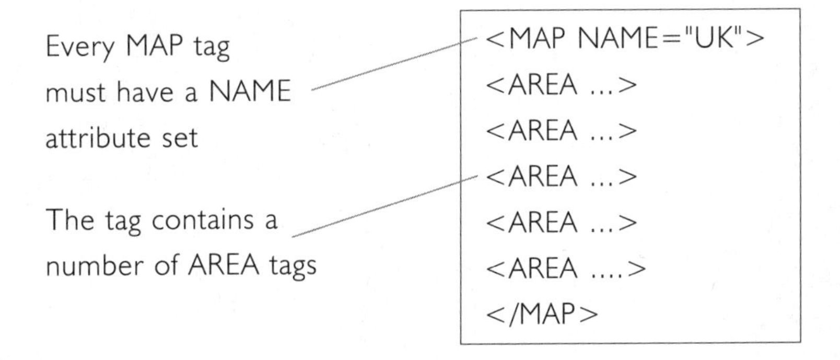

A MAP tag can be anywhere in an HTML file, but if it is placed in the BODY section it can only be referred to from that point down in the file. If you place it in the HEAD section, it can be referred to anywhere in the BODY section, which is why it's probably best to place MAP tags in the HEAD section.

You can have as many MAP tags in a file as you like, as long as they have different names. It's even possible to put all MAP tags you are using together in one HTML file (which could contain nothing else) and refer to them from other documents. Not all browsers can cope with this, though, so it's best to avoid doing it.

The AREA tags

Each AREA tag within the MAP tag should look like this:

```
<AREA SHAPE=... COORDS=... ALT=....>
```

The attributes are as follows:

SHAPE

This attribute can have possible values “RECT”, “POLY”, “CIRCLE” or “DEFAULT”. The last of these is used to give the URL to go to if the user clicks outside of the areas you have defined.

COORDS

The value of this attribute is a list of coordinates which define the area. Exactly what coordinates are given depends on the SHAPE. Rectangles have the coordinates of the top-left and bottom-right corners; circles have the coordinates of the centre and its radius. A polygon has the coordinates of each corner, however many of them it has. “Default” areas don’t have coordinates.

ALT

The ALT attribute is optional. Its value is a string which some browsers will display when you point to the area.

The IMG tag

Somewhere in the body of the HTML document you need to have an IMG tag to place your image. This should look like this:

```
<IMG SRC="uk.gif" ISMAP USEMAP="#UK">
```

There are two attributes of this tag which distinguish it from a normal IMG tag. The ISMAP attribute tells the browser to treat the image as an image map. The USEMAP attribute says what MAP tag to use. This attribute could give the complete URL of the file in which to find the MAP tag, but as mentioned above, not all browsers will handle it.

Otherwise this is an ordinary IMG tag, and you can use any other IMG attribute (ALT, ALIGN, etc.).

Server-side maps

Setting up a server-side map is a little more difficult, and depends to a certain degree on the way the server is set up.

Modern HTTP servers, such as the Netscape servers, can handle image maps themselves. In this case you need to do something like this:

```
<A HREF=uk.map><IMG SRC=uk.gif ISMAP></A>
```

The IMG tag needs to have the ISMAP attribute to tell the browser to treat it as an image map; the A tag points to the map file (and the value of the HREF attribute should point to the URL of the .map file – which need not be in the same directory or even on the same server as the HTML file).

Older servers need to use a CGI program to decode the image map. This is usually called "imagemap" or "htimage". The exact syntax to use depends on how your site's server is set up, and you will have to ask your provider for the exact syntax. One example of the syntax is:

```
<A HREF=/cgi-bin/imagemap/uk.map>
```

It can however be *much* more complicated than this – the only thing to do is to consult your local provider.

In either case you need to produce a .map file (in the correct format for your server) and place it on the server. Sometimes you can put the file in the same directory as the appropriate .html file; in other cases there is a set directory where you should put the file. Again, ask your provider.

Dual-function maps

As mentioned before, it is possible to set up an image map so that those browsers which can handle client-side maps will use that, and those that can't will use server-side.

You need to produce both a MAP tag (and edit it into your HTML file), and a .map file (which you place on the server).

The mark-up for the map itself combines the two systems we have already looked at. The tag should be something like this:

```
<A href=uk.map><IMG SRC=uk.gif ISMAP USEMAP=#UK></a>
```

The anchor should be set up as you would for a server-side map

The IMG tag should be set up as for a client-side map

If the person using your map has a browser which can handle client-side maps, it will recognise the USEMAP attribute, and ignore the anchor which surrounds the IMG tag. If the browser cannot handle client-side maps, it will ignore the USEMAP attribute, and treat the map as a client-side map. So, you get the best of both worlds!

CHAPTER SIX

Tables

HTML table syntax allows you to lay out data neatly, either to tabulate information or to control the way your pages are laid out in two dimensions.

Covers

Table syntax

The HTML to produce tables is straightforward, but it is among the most complicated areas of the language. The reason for this is that most of HTML was arrived at by a group of people adding little details to a very simple base language.

Tables, on the other hand, were the work of one person, Dave Raggett of Hewlett Packard's European research lab in Bristol, who devised the whole system. This means that it is much more logically arranged than the rest of HTML, but it is quite complicated to take in at one go.

A table consists of a number of HTML structures, nested inside one another.

- The whole table is contained between a <TABLE> and a </TABLE> tag. These tags can contain:
- An optional <CAPTION> tag;
- One or more <TR> (Table Row) tags, one for each row. Each table row can contain:
- One or more <TH> (Table Heading) or <TD> (Table Data) tags, one for each column in the table. Each of these tags can contain:
- Normal HTML code for the contents of the cell.

Each of these tags can have various attributes which affect the appearance of the table and how it is laid out, and some attributes can appear in a number of different tags, depending on the way you want it to appear.

The <TABLE> tag

The <TABLE> tag contains the whole table. It can have the following attributes:

ALIGN

The ALIGN attribute can have the values LEFT, CENTER or RIGHT. It specifies the alignment of the whole table in the browser's window – not the alignment of text in the table's cells. Normally tables are aligned to the left, unless they themselves are within a DIV or CENTER tag which specifies otherwise.

WIDTH

This specifies the table's width. If you don't supply a value for the attribute, the width of the table is worked out from the width of its contents.

You can specify the width in two different ways. WIDTH=147 will produce a table 147 pixels wide, and WIDTH="67%" will make the table 67% of the width of the browser's window.

BORDER

This attribute specifies the width of the border around the table, in pixels. If you don't set a value, the table will have no border. <TABLE BORDER> specifies a table with a border 1 pixel wide.

CELLSPACING

This attribute specifies the width of the border between individual cells of a table, and of the border between edge cells and the table border itself. Normally it has a value of 1, unless you specify CELLSPACING=0.

CELLPADDING

This specifies the space to be left between the border of each cell and its contents.

BGCOLOR

Not all browsers will honour this attribute. Those that do will use this colour as the background colour of the table. It can take the same values as the BGCOLOUR of an HTML <BODY> tag (see Chapter Three for more details).

The <CAPTION> tag

A CAPTION tag is a container – that is, you need a <CAPTION> and a </CAPTION> tag, and it affects the text between it.

The tag has one attribute, ALIGN. This can have the values TOP and BOTTOM, and specifies where the caption should be placed in relation to the table. Most browsers will normally place the caption above the table.

In general, you can only put plain text in a CAPTION tag.

Table rows

Each row of the table should be contained in a <TR> tag – that is, between a <TR> and a </TR>. The tag can have the following attributes:

ALIGN

This specifies the horizontal alignment of the contents of cells in this row. It can have the values LEFT, RIGHT or CENTER.

VALIGN

This attribute specifies the vertical alignment of the contents of cells in this row. Its possible values are TOP, MIDDLE or BOTTOM.

BGCOLOR

Not all browsers will honour this attribute. Those that do will use this colour as the background colour of the table. It can take the same values as the BGCOLOUR of an HTML <BODY> tag (see Chapter Three for more details).

Table cells

Each cell, of each row of the table, needs to be contained within a cell tag. Cell tags come in two types:

<TH>

The <TH> tag is intended for a cell which contains a heading. Text in a <TH> cell is displayed differently from that in a data cell; usually it is displayed in bold font, and the text is centred.

<TD>

This tag is used for cells which contain data. It is the usual tag you will use for cells.

Both <TH> and <TD> tags are containers; that is, the contents of the cell consists of the text between the <TD> and the </TD> tags. Unusually, the end tags are not always necessary; if the meaning is clear, you can leave them out.

The tags can have these attributes:

NOWRAP

This attribute turns off word-wrapping in the cell, so text will all appear on one line, rather than being wrapped over a number of lines. This is useful for making sure that a column is wide enough.

ROWSPAN

The value of this attribute should be a number larger than one; if you set it, the cell will span across that many rows. This is covered in more detail on page 83.

COLSPAN

This does the same as ROWSPAN, but makes the cell span a number of columns.

ALIGN

This specifies the horizontal alignment of the contents of the cell. It can have the values LEFT, CENTER or RIGHT. It will overrule the value set by an ALIGN attribute set in the <TR> tag, if there is one.

VALIGN

This attribute specifies the vertical alignment of the cell's contents. It has possible values TOP, MIDDLE and BOTTOM. It will override a VALIGN attribute set in the <TR> tag. If there is no VALIGN set for either the cell or the row, VALIGN=MIDDLE is assumed; the contents of the cell are centred between the top and bottom of the cell. This can produce some surprising results if you are not ready for it.

WIDTH

This attribute suggests the width of the cell, in pixels. It does not include the cell padding, if you have set that in the TABLE tag. If CELLPADDING is set, the actual width of the cell will be WIDTH+CELLPADDING*2.

The browser should try and follow the suggested width unless it conflicts with the width of other cells in the same column.

HEIGHT

This suggests the height of the cell in pixels, not including the cell padding. Constraints are the same as for the WIDTH attribute.

BGCOLOR

Not all browsers will honour this attribute. Those that do will use this colour as the background colour of the cell. It can take the same values as the BGCOLOUR of an HTML <BODY> tag (see Chapter Three for more details).

Cell contents

Inside each <TD> or <TH> tag, place the HTML code for the contents of the cell. You can put almost any HTML in a table cell: images, anchors, form fields, paragraphs, even other tables.

It is useful to consider the contents of a cell to be a little HTML document of its own. If you are using a non-standard font size or colour, you will need to specify it in each cell individually: it is not passed on from one cell to another.

Other HTML elements do cover more than one cell: for example, a fill-in form can contain a table, with different fields in different cells without having to repeat the <FORM> tag.

Spanning cells

Normally, a table will be laid out as a rectangular grid of cells, with the same number of cells in each row, and all the corners of the cells lining up.

There are cases when you do not wish to do this. For example, you may wish to have one heading cover a number of rows or columns. You may also want to break up the regular grid in order to produce special effects.

You can produce these effects using the COLSPAN and ROWSPAN attributes. If you start a cell with <TD COLSPAN=2>, that cell will expand to take up the space occupied by both its own column, and its neighbour on the right. In that row, you should have one less <TD> tag than usually. If you use <TD ROWSPAN=2>, the cell will expand to fill the cell immediately below it on the next row. That row should in that case have one <TD> less than usual.

Be careful when you are using spanning. It is very easy to forget to leave out a cell to make room for a spanned cell, and this will produce a "phantom column" on the right of the table. It is also possible using spanning to make two cells overlap; this is not allowed, and the results are hard to predict in advance.

Tables – an example

Let's look at this table, which we want to place on a web page:

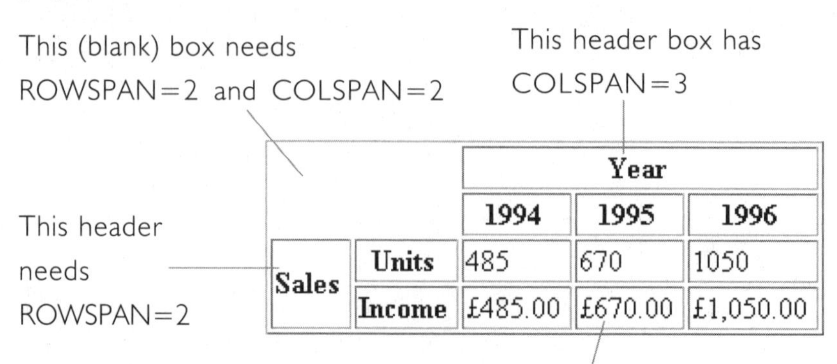

		Year		
		1994	**1995**	**1996**
Sales	**Units**	485	670	1050
	Income	£485.00	£670.00	£1,050.00

REMEMBER

The BORDER attribute here specifies that the borders of the table should be displayed. Without this, the table text would appear to be floating in space.

This is the HTML code for the top line of the table:

<TABLE BORDER>	We have to start with a <TABLE> tag
<TR>	This is the first table row
<TH ROWSPAN=2 COLSPAN=2>	This is the empty box at top-left
<TH COLSPAN=3>	This is the long box
Year	This is its contents

The code for the second line (the one that goes 1994, 1995, 1996) is like this:

If your table code is hard to follow, try indenting the self-contained sections of it in a hierarchical fashion, in order to make its structure more apparent.

<TR>	Another row in the table
<TH>	A table header cell...
1994	and its contents.
<TH>	The next cell...
1995	and its contents
<TH>	And the last...
1996	and so on...

Note that there are only three cells on this line, because of the big cell to the top left.

Now we look at the third line, which actually has some data in it:

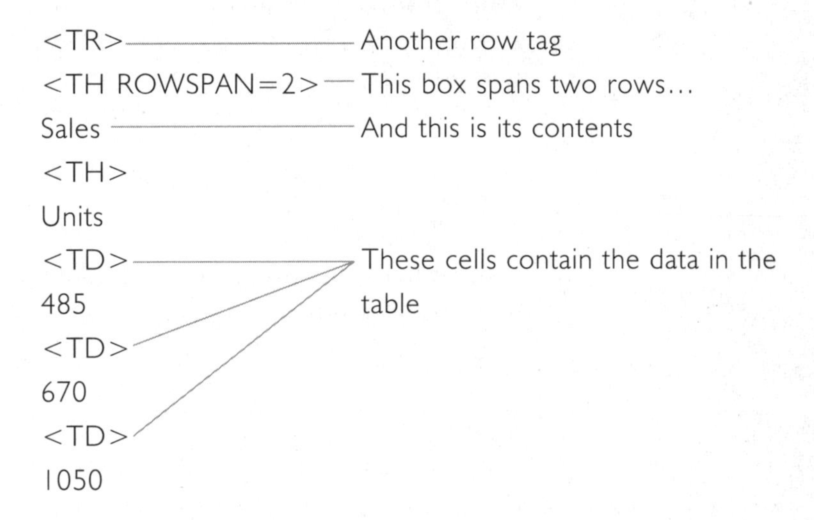

Finally, here is the mark-up for the last line of the table:

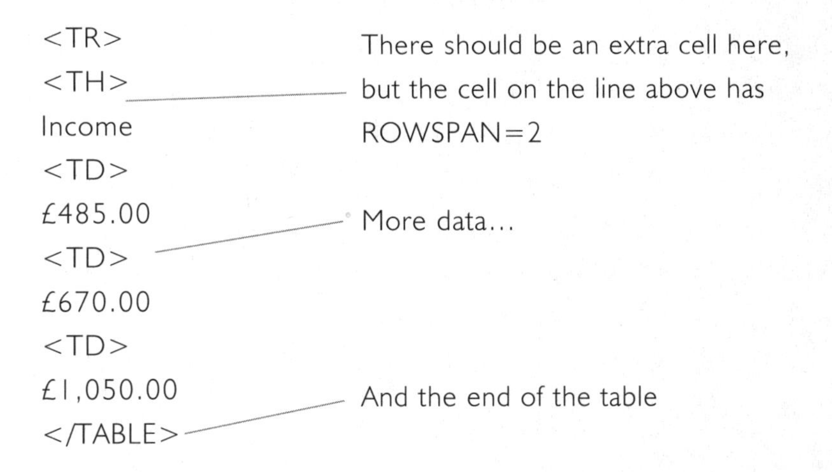

Using tables for special effects

You can use a table for other things than just neatlylaid-out information. A common use of table mark-up is to give you more control over the way objects are laid out. If a table has no border, it is not immediately obvious that you are using one; it just makes sure that images, buttons etc. are neatly laid out and that they align with their neighbours.

One common use of a table is when you are laying out a fill-in form. If you have a series of input fields one below another, normally the fields will not be aligned neatly:

It would look a lot better if the input fields were all in one column. We can do this by making up a table with two columns, with each question in the first column, and its input filed in the second. If we do that, our page looks like this:

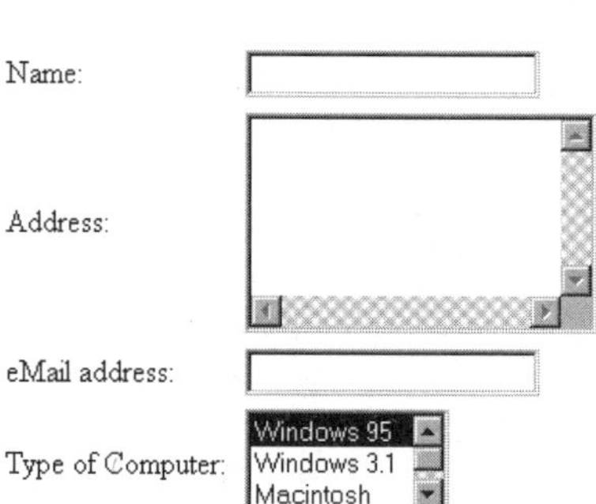

Much better, don't you think?

You can also use a table to give you a bar of icons down the left or right hand margin, or to arrange your page into a multi-column, "newspaper" layout.

CHAPTER SEVEN

Forms

There are often occasions when you need the person browsing your pages to give you information. The Fill-in Forms interface allows you to add a wide range of input devices, including text fields, menus and buttons to your web pages.

Covers

The basics

A form has two parts. Firstly, there is the part you see, the input fields which the user fills in. This consists of standard HTML mark-up, just like any other part of a web page. Secondly, there is the part which makes the form actually do something: a CGI script which extracts the information supplied by the user and processes it.

It's best to ask your provider for their instructions on setting up forms.

There is a wide range of things you can do with the form information. The simplest, and most common thing, is to lay the information out neatly, and mail it to an eMail address (for instance, to you). Most providers who allow you to set up forms (that is, most of them) provide a standard script which does this.

The next most complicated thing is to take the form information, and return a page which includes this information. For example, you could ask the user what their name is, and then produce a page addressed to them personally.

If you are working on your own server, there is really no limit to what you could do with forms. Anything which could be done with a single program running once on the server machine is possible – you could access a database to register a visitor, you could recognise individual visitors by name, you could do database searches etc. It's really up to your imagination, and your programming ability.

The <FORM> tag

The HTML part of a form consists of a <FORM> tag. The <FORM> tag contains a number of INPUT elements, which provide the actual fields in which to enter data. Unlike some other HTML elements, you can put any other mark-up within the <FORM> tag – as far as the form is concerned, as long as you have a <FORM> and a </FORM> tag, and some INPUT elements, that's all that matters. A form can be as large as you like – you could put the tags at the beginning and the end of the BODY section of your HTML file, if you wanted to, and it would work just the same. You can have more than one form on a page, as long as they don't overlap. You also cannot have a form inside another one.

The <FORM> tag has a number of attributes:

It is possible for you to submit a form by eMail, avoiding the need for producing a CGI script. There are some limitations to this approach, and it is quite complicated, so this option will be covered in its own section later, on pages 98-100.

ACTION

The ACTION attribute tells the form what to do with the data when the form is submitted. Normally the value of this attribute should be the URL of the CGI script which will process this form. The exact syntax of this depends on how your web server is set up. See Chapter Eleven for more details.

METHOD

There are two ways for the browser to send the information to the web server. Which one to use is determined by the METHOD attribute. These options are:

METHOD=POST

This is the method you should use under normal circumstances. It opens the connection to the CGI script on the other end, and then sends the form information. As far as the script is concerned, the form data can be read on its standard input (if you don't understand what this means, don't worry!)

METHOD=GET

This method sends the information in the same way as normal CGI scripts are supplied with information – the data is encoded into the URL with which it is called. For a number of reasons (not least that the information you have typed into the form is easily visible while in transit), you should not usually use this method.

Annoyingly, if you don't specify a METHOD attribute, it defaults to GET. So you should *always* specify METHOD=POST.

Input fields

A FORM tag itself does not change the appearance of the web page on which it appears. The visible part of a form is provided by the INPUT, SELECT and TEXTAREA tags which are contained within it.

INPUT tags are used for producing single-line text fields, password fields, check boxes, radio buttons, submit and reset buttons, hidden fields, file upload and image buttons. SELECT tags are used for menus. TEXTAREA tags are used to define multi-area text fields.

Of these tags, TEXTAREA and SELECT are containers – i.e., they have start and end tags. There is no </INPUT> tag.

All input tags have a NAME attribute, which is how their values are passed on when the form is submitted. You must always remember to give all your fields a name – otherwise the field won't show up and you might as well not include it. Be careful: this is an easy mistake to make.

The type of Input field displayed by an INPUT tag depends on the value of the TYPE attribute. Possible values are:

TYPE=TEXT

This is the input device you will get if you don't specify a TYPE attribute. A TEXT input looks like this:

The TEXT input can have these attributes:

SIZE

This defines the visible length of the field, in characters.

A user can type more than this by scrolling in the window.

MAXLENGTH

This defines the maximum possible number of characters that a user can put in the field.

VALUE

The value of the, er, VALUE attribute, should you choose to set it, should be a string. The initial value of the input field will be set to this string.

TYPE=PASSWORD

This type of input looks exactly like a TEXT input, except when the user types into it, each character shows up as a "*". This is to stop prying eyes looking over the user's shoulder when they are entering a password.

TYPE=CHECKBOX

A CHECKBOX input looks like this: ☑

This input type can be used for two purposes. Firstly, it can be used for an option which can either be on or off. Secondly, it can be used for an input field which can have none, one or more of a number of different values.

In the first case you simply have a single INPUT tag:

```
<INPUT TYPE=CHECKBOX NAME=cooked VALUE=yes>
```

If this is selected, then when the form is submitted, you will get the value "cooked=yes".

For the second case you should have a number of CHECKBOX tags, all with the same name, but with different VALUE settings.

If a CHECKBOX input has the CHECKED attribute set, it will be displayed initially in a checked state.

This HTML code...

```
Toppings: <BR>
Ham <INPUT TYPE=CHECKBOX
  NAME=toppings VALUE=ham><BR>
Mushroom <INPUT TYPE=CHECKBOX
  NAME=toppings VALUE=mushroom><BR>
Pineapple <INPUT TYPE=CHECKBOX
  NAME=toppings VALUE=pineapple><BR>
```

...will look like this in a browser

Toppings:
Ham ☐
Mushroom ☐
Pineapple ☐

TYPE=RADIO

This input type is used when an attribute should have one (and only one) of a limited range of options.

A single button looks like this: ◉

It's called a "radio button", by the way, because it works like the buttons on a car radio where one button is pressed in at a time: if you press a button, the one that's already pressed pops out.

You should have a different RADIO tag for each option you want, all with the NAME attribute set to the same value. Each tag should have a different value for the VALUE attribute. One of the tags should have the CHECKED attribute set.

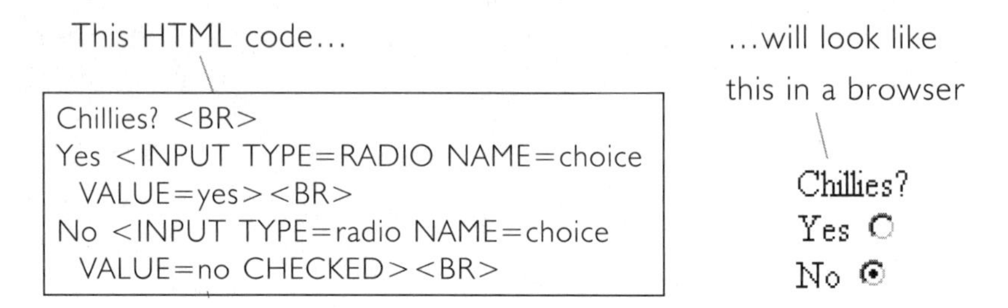

TYPE=SUBMIT

This input type produces a button to submit the form to the web server.

A SUBMIT input looks like this: Submit Query

If you set the VALUE attribute of the tag, this will be the text written on the button. If you also set the NAME attribute, then the name-value pair will be sent to the server. This is useful because you can have more than one SUBMIT button, and you may want to know which one the user has pressed.

If you don't want rectangular grey buttons with text in them, use the next input type:

TYPE=IMAGE

This input type is basically a SUBMIT button, but uses a graphic rather than the normal rectangular grey box. It should have SRC and ALIGN attributes set, just like an IMG tag.

NAME and VALUE attributes are treated like a SUBMIT input, and you should at least set the VALUE attribute, in case the user doesn't have a graphical browser (or in case they have Download Graphics turned off).

TYPE=RESET

This input type looks like this:

If the button is pressed, the values of all fields in the form are reset to the state they were in when the form was first displayed.

You can set the message on the button using the VALUE attribute.

Reset buttons don't supply any data, so no information is sent when the form is submitted.

A warning about this input type: I have never seen anyone use it on a web page, and it would be quite tricky in programming terms to write a CGI script to handle it.

TYPE=FILE

It is intended to allow a user to specify a file on their local disk to be submitted to the form.

The input field looks like this:

The user can either type a file name directly into the text box, or they can press the "Browse..." button and a file selector will pop up and they can choose a file.

You can use the SIZE and MAXLENGTH attributes to limit the size of the text field, and the ACCEPT attribute to control the type of file the user can give. Beyond that, you're in guru territory.

TYPE=HIDDEN

The HIDDEN input does not show up on a form, and the user has no way to alter it. Its NAME and VALUE attributes are returned as usual when the form is submitted.

You may be puzzled why you can have an input type to which you can provide no input. The reason is this: in general, a form is "stateless"; that is, there is no way for the CGI script to tell that you have previously filled in some other form, or have in the past registered with a service, or anything else. The script is just run: it runs, it finishes, and that is the end of it.

A hidden field allows you to place information from a previous form, or information which may already be on the server, in a form. To do this, it is necessary for the form to be generated dynamically – that is, rather than the form being a static HTML document, it is produced as the output of a CGI script, with the value of the hidden field or fields worked out at the time the CGI script is run. For example, you may have a long list of questions to ask the user, and you want to split the form into a number of shorter pages. The first page of questions is a normal HTML file. When it is submitted, it runs a CGI script whose output is the form asking a second set of questions, with the answers to the first set placed in hidden fields in the form. When this form is submitted it may produce a third form, and so on until you finally run a script to process all the results.

There are two ways to pass information through hidden fields. The simpler, but less neat way is to simply reproduce the data in hidden fields, so your form contains a group of tags like this:

```
<INPUT TYPE=HIDDEN NAME=FNAME VALUE="Andy">
```

This approach is easy to do, and works well, but anyone looking at the source of a form can find out what the data is – which you may not want to happen!

The neater way to use hidden inputs to pass information is to use what is known as a "Cookie" (it may or may not say something about the maturity of the average hacker that the name is derived from the Cookie Monster from Sesame Street!). The method works like this: when you are given the first bit of information to identify a particular user, you store this in a database of some type, and get back a number (or suchlike) with which you can fetch that record in the database later (in database terms, this is referred to as a "key", which shows that database programmers watch less children's television than network programmers). On the next screen, you place this key in a hidden field. When the next form is processed, you can place the new information in the same record as the old stuff.

This approach is very useful if you keep a lot of information on individual people – you might have their name, eMail address, home address, fax number, phone number, date of first contact, list of all the times they have contacted you, and so on. Besides the fact that it's not a great idea to send all this stuff plainly readable over the Internet too often, if you have all this information in hidden fields your form will take an age to process, and your service will look a lot worse than it really is.

HANDY TIP

See Chapter Eleven for details of where to get PERL.

You can use this effect without needing a commercial database package: there is a library available in PERL which will read and write data files in the "dbm" format, and this is quite adequate as long as you won't be processing too many people at once. The dbm libraries are part of the normal PERL distribution, and there are packages to handle the same format in several other languages.

SELECT tags

The SELECT tag is used to define one-from-many and many-from-many menus.

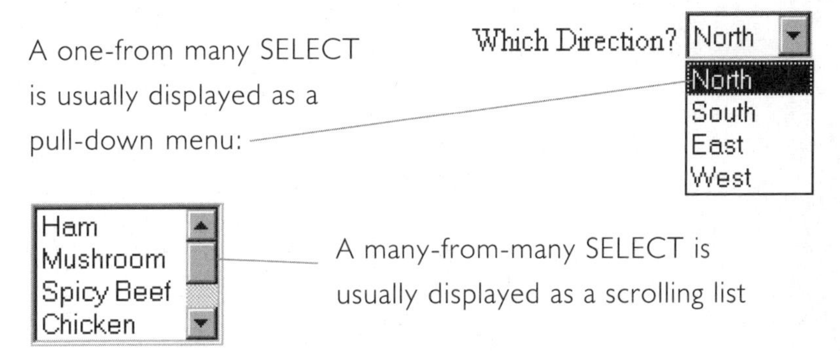

A one-from many SELECT is usually displayed as a pull-down menu:

A many-from-many SELECT is usually displayed as a scrolling list

A SELECT tag needs both a start and an end tag. It contains one or more <OPTION> tags (which do not have an end tag). Each OPTION tag takes up one line, and the text on the rest of the line is used as the label for that line of the menu.

The SELECT tag has these attributes:

NAME
This specifies the name to be passed when the form is submitted, like the NAME attribute of the other inputs.

SIZE
This specifies the number of lines to be shown in the window of a scrolling list.

MULTIPLE
If this attribute is set, then the tag allows many-of-many selections. If not, only one-of-many is allowed.

The OPTION tags can have these attributes:

SELECTED
If this attribute is selected, then this option is initially selected when the form is loaded.

VALUE
This is the value returned if this line is selected.

The TEXTAREA tag

The TEXTAREA tag produces a multiple-line text-input box. A TEXTAREA tag needs both a start and an end tag.

Anything in the HTML between the start and end tags will be used as the initial value of the input field.

The TEXTAREA tag can have these attributes:

NAME
This gives the name to return, just like other input types.

ROWS
This attribute defines how big to display the input field on the screen. It is possible to type more rows than this into the box; if the user does, then the browser will display a scroll bar on the box.

COLS
This attribute defines how wide the input box should be, in characters. It is possible to type in longer lines than this; some browsers will wrap the text, others will give the input box a scroll bar.

Submitting a form

When your form's submit button is pressed, the CGI script specified in the form's ACTION attribute is run.

If the form's METHOD attribute is set to "GET", the contents of the input fields of the form are sent in the normal CGI manner – that is, they are encoded in the HTTP request after the address of the CGI script. If the form has METHOD=POST, then the result of the form is sent following the HTTP request – the CGI script can read the data on its standard input. For a number of boring and technical reasons, you should usually use METHOD=POST.

If you are lucky, you will not need to write your own CGI script to process your form. Most service providers will have a selection of sample scripts which you can either use without modification, or which you can easily edit for your particular purposes.

Ask your provider for this script.

The single most common thing which people use forms for is to set up a feedback or enquiry form. The user fills in this form, and the results are formatted up, and eMailed to a particular eMail address. Most providers have a script to do this, and at the most you will need to edit the script to put your eMail address in the relevant place.

If you want to do something more elaborate you will have to produce your own script. For a collection of suitable scripts, try the **cgi-lib** PERL library, which does most of the messy bits of handling forms for you (and comes with a nice step-by-step guide to putting your form together and writing the script). You can find the library on the Internet at:

http://www.bio.cam.ac.uk/cgi-lib/

Submitting a form by eMail

It is possible to set up a form to send its results by eMail. To do this, you have to stick to two things:

- The form's method must be POST;
- The ACTION attribute should be a mailto: URL (see Chapter Two if you're not sure about what a mailto: URL is).

An eMail form is good to test your form, but it has a couple of problems. Firstly, there is no way you can get an immediate result to a form (all eMail can take a minute or two to be sent). Secondly, sending form data by eMail is a security risk, and Netscape warns you of this fact:

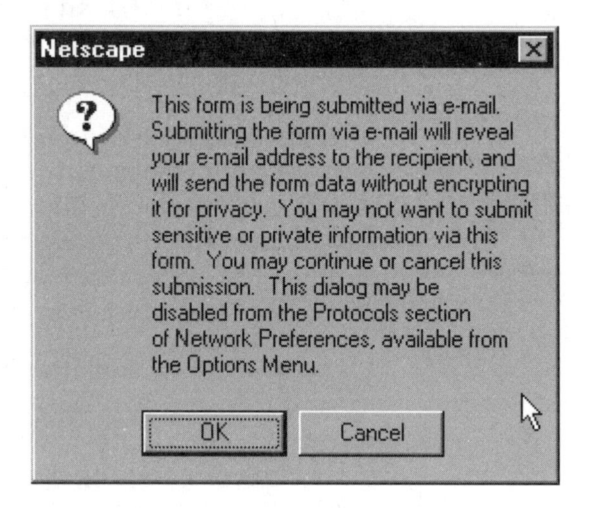

This security risk may mean that large organisations will not let their users use this type of form at all.

If the user goes through with it and sends the mail, you then get an eMail with the values of the form attached as a text file. It is then up to you to edit this into a usable form.

It would be possible to run a "visitors' book" page like this, but a script would be both more secure and efficient.

Forms – an example

Here is an example of a piece of a form, taken from Computer Step's web site, that requests information from the user, who can then press a button to submit the contents of the form via eMail (see the previous page).

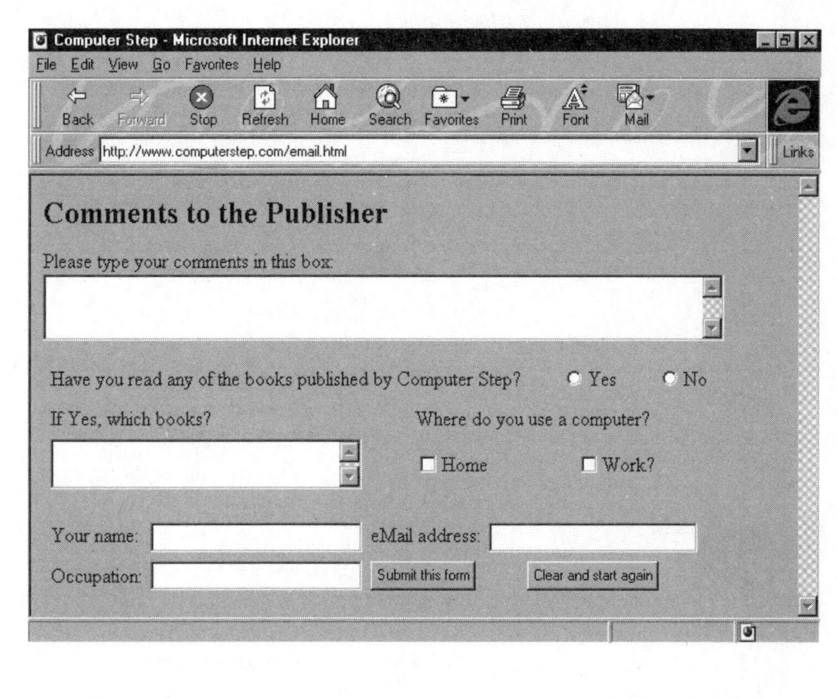


```
<html>
<title>Computer Step</title>
<body>
```

Sets the document title and begins the body text

```
<h2>Comments to the Publisher</h2>
```

Sets the heading

```
<form method=post
action="mailto:publisher@computerstep.com">
```

Sets the email destination

```
<p>Please type your comments in this box:<br>
<textarea name="comments" rows=2 cols=110>
</textarea>
```

Sets text area of 2 rows, 110 columns

```
<p><table cellspacing=5 width=95%>
<tr>
	<td>Have you read any of the books
published by Computer Step?</td>
```

Defines a table to organise layout of question and radio buttons

```
        <td><input name="yesnoreadbooks"
type=radio>Yes</td>
        <td><input name="yesnoreadbooks"
type=radio>No</td>
</tr>
</table>
```

(...contd) Defines radio buttons (note: both have same name)

```
<table cellspacing=5 width=95%>
<tr>
        <td>If Yes, which books?</td>
        <td colspan=2>Where do you use a
computer?</td>
</tr><tr>
        <td><textarea name="readbooks" rows=1
cols=50></textarea></td>
        <td><input name="compathome"
type=checkbox>Home</td>
        <td><input name="compatwork"
type=checkbox>Work?</td>
</tr>
</table>
```

Defines a table to organise the layout of the questions, text areas and check-boxes

```
<p><table cellspacing=5>
<tr valign="top">
        <td>Your name:</td>
        <td><input name="name" size=30></td>
        <td>eMail address:</td>
        <td><input name="email" size=30></
textarea></td>
</tr><tr>
        <td>Occupation:</td>
        <td><input name="occupation"
size=30></td>
```

Defines a table to organise the layout of the questions and text boxes for the input of name, eMail and occupation...

```
        <td><input type="submit" value="Submit
this form"></td>
        <td align="center"><input type="reset"
value="Clear and start again"></td>
</tr>
```

...and the buttons that submit the form, or clear its contents

```
</table>
```

Closes the table

```
</form>
</body>
</html>
```

Closes the form, body text and the html content

CHAPTER EIGHT

Frames

Using frames allows you to divide the browser window into a number of independent windows. This makes it easy to provide button bars, etc., which scroll differently from the main HTML document.

Covers

The basics

Normally, a browser will display a single HTML document in its window. Using the frames extensions to HTML, you can divide the main browser window into a number of sub-windows, referred to as "frames". Each frame has separate scroll bars, etc.

Each frame contains a different HTML document, and links in one frame can affect the document displayed in other ones.

Frames can have a number of uses. One of the more useful is to allow you to put all the standard links which you would have at the top or bottom of each page in a window of their own, which doesn't scroll. Then, no matter where in your HTML file the user is looking, they still have easy access to these links.

You should approach frames with a certain amount of caution. Firstly, not all web browsers can handle frames. You should always provide a non-framed version of any pages which use frames. Secondly, a document using frames will display significantly slower than an equivalent document which does not use frames. This is partly because each frame is a separate HTML file, which has to be fetched from the server, but more importantly because browsers seem to display pages much more slowly if they are in a frame than if they are the only page in a window. Framed documents are often a cause of crashing browsers.

For these reasons, a lot of Internet users are biased against frames. When you are designing a document, don't use frames just because they are there or because everyone else is using them: only use them if there is a pressing need for them, and in any case always provide a way to access the same data without using them.

Frame syntax

A framed document is like any other HTML document, with one exception: instead of a <BODY> tag (which contains the body of the document), it has a <FRAMESET> tag, which lists the HTML documents which will make up the page.

The <FRAMESET> tag

This is the main container of a framed document. Between the <FRAMESET> tag and the </FRAMESET> tag, you can only have other FRAMESET tags, FRAME tags or the NOFRAMES tag. If any other normal BODY-type mark-up tags are used between the FRAMESET tags, then the FRAMESET command is ignored.

The FRAMESET tag has two attributes:

ROWS

The value of the ROWS attribute is a series of values, separated by commas. These values determine how the screen is to be divided up between different frames. There are three ways of expressing these values, and you can mix them in a single ROWS attribute.

The simplest way is to just put a number, which will be the height of that frame in pixels. This is a dangerous approach to take for a complete frameset, because screens vary in size: just because your screen is 480 pixels high, it doesn't mean everybody's screen is that size.

The next method is to express the size as a percentage, in which case that frame will be assigned that percentage of the available space. You can specify percentages over 100%: in that case all percentages are scaled down. If percentages are less than 100%, then extra space will be given to any relative-sized frames (see below), and if there are no relative-sized frames then all percentages are scaled up.

The final method is to use what are called "relative-sized" frames. Use a "*" for the frame size, and this frame will be assigned any remaining space after any absolute or percentage frames have been taken care of. Extra space is divided between any relative-sized frames. You can put a number before the "*" to give that frame a larger share of extra space. For example "2*,*" defines two frames, one taking two-thirds of available space, the other one third.

Here is an example frameset tag:

```
<FRAMESET ROWS="10%,*">
```

This defines two frames, one taking up the top ten percent of the window height, the other what is left.

```
<FRAMESET ROWS="30,*,2*,15%">
```

This describes four frames. The top one is 30 pixels high, the bottom one is 15% of the window, and the other two divide up what is left in proportions of 2/3 and 1/3.

COLS

This attribute has the same syntax as the ROWS attribute, but divides the screen up horizontally.

A FRAMESET tag can have either the ROWS or the COLS attribute assigned, but not both. To have both vertical and horizontal divisions on the same page, put a second FRAMESET tag inside the other.

For example, suppose we want a box down the left-hand side of the screen, 100 pixels wide (for a row of buttons). In the right-hand part of the screen, we want a large box at the top, for the main information on the page, and a smaller box at the bottom for commentary. We would use this HTML:

```
<FRAMESET COLS="100,*">
<FRAME>
<FRAMESET ROWS="*,20%">
...
</FRAMESET>
</FRAMESET>
```

This would produce this layout:

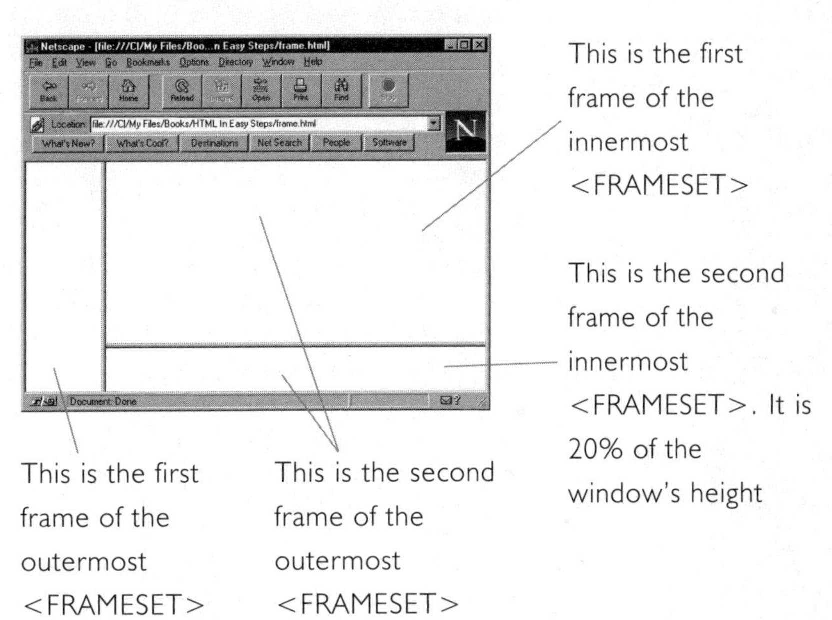

The <FRAME> tag

This tag describes the individual frames within a <FRAMESET> tag. It is not a container, so there is no </FRAME> tag. The <FRAME> tag has the following attributes:

SRC

The value of the SRC attribute is the URL of the HTML file to place in this frame. If you have no SRC attribute, the browser will display a blank frame.

NAME

This attribute is used to give a frame a name, so that it can be addressed by links in other documents (usually in other frames in the same window). We'll go through targeting links later in this chapter.

MARGINWIDTH

The value of this attribute is the horizontal distance in pixels between the contents of the frame and the left and right edges of the frame itself.

The minimum MARGINWIDTH is 1 – that is, there must be a gap between the edge of a cell and its contents.

MARGINHEIGHT

This is just like the MARGINWIDTH attribute, except it affects the top and bottom margins instead of the left and right ones.

SCROLLING

This attribute determines whether the frame should have scrollbars or not. SCROLLING=YES means that the frame will always have scrollbars, SCROLLING=NO means that it will never have scrollbars, and SCROLLING=AUTO leaves it to the browser to decide whether or not the frame should have scrollbars. This is the only way, by the way, to have one scrollbar (say the vertical one) but not the other one (say the horizontal).

If you don't specify the value of the SCROLLING attribute, it's assumed to be "auto".

NORESIZE

Normally, the user can change the sizes of individual frames by dragging them with the mouse. There are times when you don't want this to happen – when a frame contains a set of buttons which have a particular size, for example. In this case, set the NORESIZE attribute, and that frame will not be resizable.

The <NOFRAMES> tag

Some people who want to view your pages will not have a browser which can handle frames. For their benefit, you should put some HTML code between the <NOFRAMES> and the </NOFRAMES> tags, which either presents the same information without using frames, or which points to a non-framed version of your page. A browser which can handle frames will ignore anything contained by the NOFRAMES tag; one which cannot handle frames will see nothing else. Some people will not want to use frames, so you should always put in a link to a non-framed version of your page.

Using the TARGET attribute

In normal HTML, when you click on a link, the result of following that link appears in the same window. When we have multiple windows in which documents can appear (as we do in a document using frames) we need a way to tell the browser that the results of clicking on a link should appear in a different window. We can do this using a set of extensions to HTML which involve the TARGET attribute.

You can use the TARGET extensions to HTML in other situations than just frames (for example, you can open another browser window which will act as a "remote control"), but they are most useful when you're working with frames.

There are two parts to the TARGET extensions. Firstly, you need to be able to give a particular window a name, and secondly, you need to tell the browser that the results of a request should go to a named window.

Naming windows

There are three ways of giving a particular window a name. Firstly, the document can be sent with this HTTP header:

```
Window-target: window-name
```

You can set extra HTTP headers using the <META> tag in the document's HEAD region.

Secondly, if a document is fetched via a link with the TARGET attribute set, a window with that name will be created if one does not already exist.

Thirdly, and most importantly in the context of frames, a FRAME tag can have the NAME attribute set, which will assign that name to that frame's window.

Using the TARGET attribute in a link

You can use the TARGET attribute in a variety of HTML tags. In all these cases the value of the TARGET attribute should be the name of the required window.

TARGET in an A tag

You can add the TARGET attribute to a normal anchor tag.

When the anchor is clicked on, the document will appear in the named window.

TARGET in a BASE tag

You should use this approach when all (or most) links in a document should go to a particular window. Using <BASE TARGET="mywindow"> will mean that all links in the document which do not themselves have a different TARGET attribute set will be displayed in the window named “mywindow”.

TARGET in an AREA tag

The AREA tag is used in a client-side image map's MAP tag. See Chapter Five for more details. When the hot-spot specified by the AREA tag is clicked on, the linked document will be displayed in the window named by the TARGET tag.

TARGET in a FORM tag

The FORM tag is used to define a fill-in form. See Chapter Seven for more details. The TARGET attribute will make the result of submitting the form be displayed in the named window.

TARGET names

Names which you assign should always start with a letter or a number. In addition, there are a number of special names which you can use. These names all start with an underline character, "_".

TARGET="_blank"

This link will be displayed in a new window which does not have a window name.

TARGET="_self"

The result of this link will always be loaded in the same window as the link is displayed.

TARGET="_parent"

The result of this link will be displayed in the immediate parent of the current window. That is, if the current window is a frame, it will be displayed in the window of the

FRAMESET document which contains this FRAME tag. If the current window does not have a parent, it is treated as a TARGET="_self".

TARGET="_top"
This link will always be displayed in the full browser window, regardless of how many layers of FRAMESET tags we are down.

Frames – an example

Below is an example of the use of frames, taken from Computer Step's web page. This uses two frames – one to hold the links bar you see at the top of the browser window, and another, larger frame for the main view. One of the advantages of using frames for HTML content that takes up more than one page is that the links bar always appears at the top of the page, no matter how far down the main body of the page the viewer scrolls. This is much more convenient than having to scroll back up to the top of the page every time you want to link to another page.

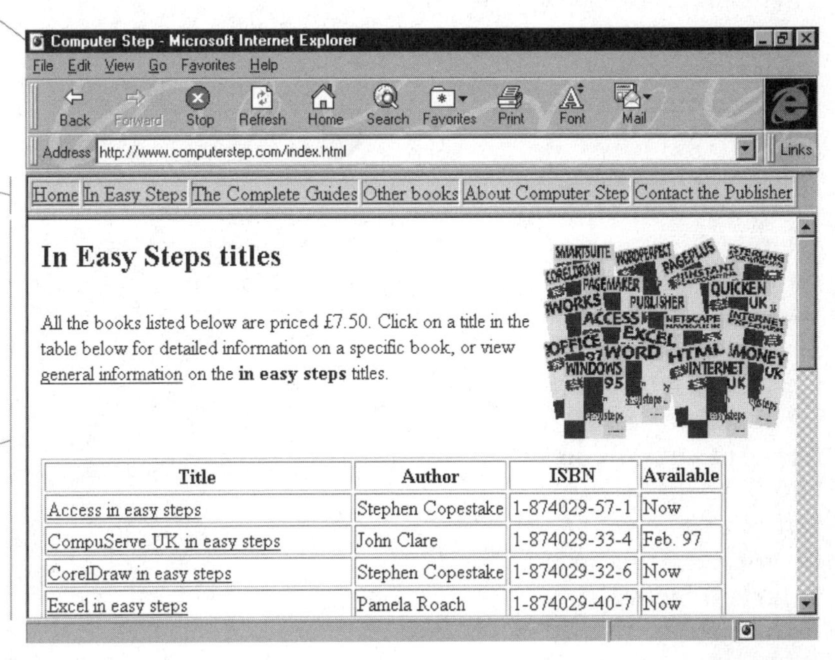

This shows a browser whose window has been split into two frames by the "index.html" file that is given on the following page

This frame, occupying 9% of the height of the browser's window, holds the links bar created by the "buttons.html" file, overleaf

This, frame, named "main_window" in the "index.html" file, fills the remaining 91% of the height of the browser's window. It is currently displaying the "easystep.html" page, which has been selected from the links bar

The first HTML file here, called “index.html”, is the file that the browser first opens when it is pointed at the site.

```
<html>
<head><title>Computer Step</title></head>
<frameset rows="9%,*">
  <frame src="buttons.html" marginheight=0
  marginwidth=0 noresize>
  <frame src="home.html" name="main_window">

  <noframes>
    Sorry, this browser does not support frames.
    <a href="home.html">Click here</a> to
    link to the home page.
  </noframes>
</frameset>
</html>
```

Opens the HTML file

Sets 2 rows, 9% and 91% of the window's height

Allocates top row to buttons.html

Allocates bottom row to home.html

Allows people with unsuitable browsers to link to home page

Closes frameset & HTML

Every anchor in this table contains the command *target="main_window"*. This causes every referenced HTML document to be displayed not in the frame from which it was called (the top one), but in the frame which was named “main_ window” in the “index.html” file – i.e., the bottom one.

The home page appears initially in the bottom frame, but is then replaced by whatever page is selected from the links bar.

This HTML file, “buttons.html”, produces the links bar which appears in the top frame:

```
<html>
<head><title>Computer Step</title></head>
<body>
<table border cellpadding=0 align="center"
bgcolor="dddddd">
<tr bgcolor="dddddd">
  <td><a href="home.html" target=
  "main_window">Home</a></td>
  <td><a href="easystep.html" target=
  "main_window">In Easy Steps</a></td>
  <td><a href="complete.html" target=
  "main_window">The Complete Guides</a></td>
  <td><a href="others.html" target=
  "main_window">Other books</a></td>
  <td><a href="aboutcs.html" target=
  "main_window">About Computer Step</a></td>
  <td><a href="email.html" target=
  "main_window">Contact the Publisher</a></td>
</tr>
</table></body>
</html>
```

Opens the HTML file/body area

Sets a table with a grey background

Each entry between the <td>...</td> tags constitutes one cell of the one-row table, each cell containing a link to another HTML document

Closes the table/body area/HTML

CHAPTER NINE

Sound and Video

As well as HTML and images, it is possible to add sound and video to your web pages. This chapter explains a number of ways to do this.

Covers

Background sounds

You can place a sound file (a .wav or a .mid file is usually best) on a web page by simply placing an <A> tag with the sound file as its HREF. When the anchor is clicked on, the sound will be downloaded, and if the viewer's computer can play that sort of sound, it will be played.

Microsoft Internet Explorer allows you to do something a bit more interesting: you can specify a sound which will be played when the page is displayed. The sound file can be played once, a number of times, or can be set to play continuously for as long as the page is displayed. You do this using the <BGSOUND> tag.

The <BGSOUND> tag is not a container – that is, you don't have to finish it with a </BGSOUND> tag. For best results, you should place it in the <HEAD> region of your document. It has two possible attributes:

LOOP

This attribute specifies how many times the sound should be played. That is, LOOP=3 will play the sound three times. If you specify LOOP=INFINITE, then the sound will play for as long as the page is displayed.

SRC

The value of the SRC attribute should be the URL of the sound file which you wish to play.

The <BGSOUND> tag is only recognised by Microsoft Internet Explorer; all other browsers ignore it, and someone looking at your page using Netscape Navigator, for instance, will hear nothing.

RealAudio

Virgin radio transmit 24 hours a day using Real Audio. Look at www.virginradio.co.uk to try it out.

If you link an ordinary sound file to a web page, someone downloading the sound will have to wait for the entire file to arrive before they can hear the sound. This can be tedious if your sound sample is more than a few seconds long. RealAudio provides an alternative. The RealAudio plug-in opens a connection over the Internet to a server, and plays sound as it arrives. This allows complete radio shows to be accessible from a web page, and it is even possible to transmit live audio. As long as the user keeps a connection to the Internet, the sound keeps on arriving.

To deliver RealAudio on your web page, you need access to a RealAudio server. This is a special program, a bit like a http server, which you can buy from Progressive Networks – the producers of RealAudio. If you have your own web server with a direct connection to the net, this is fine: if not, you can rent channels on public servers, rather like renting web space. Each channel allows one person to listen to your output; if you rent five channels, that allows a maximum of five people to simultaneously listen in.

You can get all the software associated with RealAudio from Progressive Networks' web site:

http://www.realaudio.com

To put out sound files using RealAudio, they need to be converted into a special format. Progressive Networks produces an encoder which will do this for you. There are two versions of this encoder. There is a free version which you can download from the web site, and a version which is included when you buy a RealAudio server. The paid-for version will encode live sound sources. There are versions of the encoder for Windows, Macintosh and Unix systems.

Placing RealAudio files on your pages

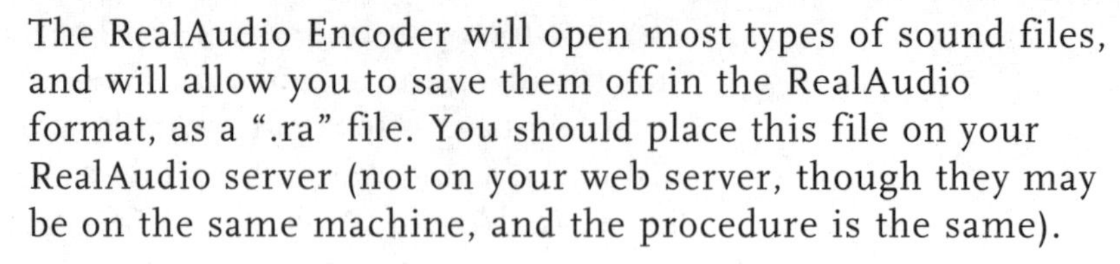

The RealAudio Encoder will open most types of sound files, and will allow you to save them off in the RealAudio format, as a ".ra" file. You should place this file on your RealAudio server (not on your web server, though they may be on the same machine, and the procedure is the same).

You can save .ra files in a number of different resolutions, depending on the speed of connection which will be used.

To link this file to your HTML files, you need to create a "RealAudio Metafile". This file tells the RealAudio player which server to contact, and which file to ask for. RealAudio Metafiles have a ".ram" file type.

You can prepare a metafile using a text editor. It consists of one or more lines, each containing the URL of a ".ra" file. If you have more than one line in your metafile, the RealAudio player will play each file in turn, and the user can move forward and back between the files.

The URL of a RealAudio file is just like a normal URL, except it uses a special service type: "pnm", which stands for "Progressive Networks Metafile".

Suppose, for example, you had rented space on a RealAudio Server at www.sound.co.uk, and had placed the file "hello.ra" in the directory "myspace".

To attach this to your home page, you would do the following:

1. Create a file called "hello.ram". The contents of the file would be:

   pnm://www.sound.co.uk/myspace/hello.ra

2. Copy "hello.ram" to your web server

3. In your HTML file, put this link:

   <A HREF=hello.ram>Hello, World!</A>

And that's all there is to it!

Video

While animated GIF images are popular, especially on large, professionally designed web sites, it's quite possible to spend hours freely surfing the web without seeing a single page containing true video. The main reason for this is that video files are usually very large, and can take an annoyingly long time to download, especially if a slow modem is being used to access a busy web site. The video files you are likely to find on the Internet are usually in .AVI or .MOV format.

Audio Video Interleave files are the standard Video for Windows format, while QuickTime movies, with the extension .MOV, are native to the Apple Macintosh – though if you have a multimedia-capable PC or Mac, you may well have utilities for both formats.

Incorporating video into your web site is as easy as displaying a still image, but ensuring that others will be able to view your video is a different matter, owing to the idiosyncrasies of different browsers, and to the fact that not everyone will necessarily have all of the appropriate video-playing utilities. You have two basic options, as follows.

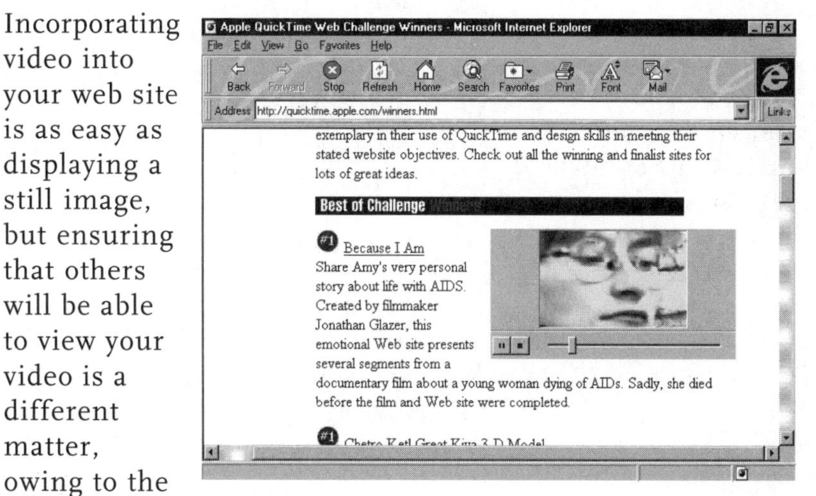

One method of inserting a video reference into an HTML file is simply to link to it as you would to another HTML file. For example, consider the following code from a normal HTML document:

```
<A HREF="rover.avi">Click here </A>to see a short
film of me walking my dog.
```

Clicking on the text link "Click here" would cause your browser to open your .AVI player utility (if you have one), and begin playing the movie. Similarly, a reference to "rover.mov" would open your QuickTime player.

The problem with this method is that the web site designer cannot dictate where on the screen the movie plays, when it plays, or what size its window is, since the video player is not directly controlled by the browser, but is merely summoned by it. It would seem more in keeping with the overall philosophy of web page design, then, if a video could be placed directly on a page, and manipulated, just as if it were an image, using the <IMG> tag. This is possible in Microsoft Internet Explorer, but not in Netscape Navigator up to v3. A lot of people use early versions of Navigator, so you would be right to be wary of excluding it for displaying video. However, should you decide to include an in-line video clip, you need to use the attribute DYNSRC after the <IMG> tag, and you are limited to using .AVI files. For example:

```
<IMG DYNSRC="rover.avi">
```

This would place the movie (assuming that it is located in the same directory as the HTML file) at its default size, directly below whatever was placed before it in the HTML file. However, you can adjust its placement, size, etc., just as you would a still image. The following code:

```
<IMG DYNSRC="rover.avi" ALIGN="center">
```

...would place the movie mid-way between the browser's left and right margins.

There are several attributes you can use in relation to this feature, which are placed within the same brackets as the IMG tag. If you want to display buttons allowing the user to stop, start and browse through the movie, add the attribute "CONTROLS". By default, the movie will play once and then stop, but to modify this, use the attribute "LOOP=", followed by a number or the word"INFINITE". For example, the following will display our movie with control buttons, and play it five times:

```
<IMG DYNSRC="rover.avi" CONTROLS LOOP=5>
```

CHAPTER TEN

Active Content

All the examples of HTML we have looked at elsewhere in this book are "static" – they do nothing until you do, and the interaction is limited by the constraints of HTML. There are a number of methods to add other types of interaction to a web site, which are described in this chapter.

Covers

Types of active content

There are a number of different technologies to provide some type of active content. One of the oldest is “server push”, in which instead of sending a single web page from the server, you send a series of pages one after another. This can give the effect of a page animating without any intervention from the user. A variation on this is “client pull”, which does the same thing except it tells the browser to request pages one after another.

The next level of sophistication is using “plug-ins”, which allow you to display and manipulate unusual data formats on a web page. There are plug-ins to handle real-time sound, video, virtual reality, and (most famously) Macromedia Director files.

The trendiest and most over-hyped technology on the Internet is Java. This is a programming language designed to support network computers by sending software over the Internet rather than storing it on hard disk. You can display certain Java programs, called “applets” on a web page. At the moment everybody wants some Java on their web page, but something is yet to be created in Java which lives up to all the hysteria.

Netscape has produced an interpreted subset of Java, called “JavaScript”, which can be programmed into an HTML document.

Microsoft, as usual, responded to Java by coming up with its own system, called “ActiveX”. This is based on “OLE”, which is the way you can link part of a Word document into Excel, etc. The big difference is in security: Java has some fairly stringent security arrangements, designed to prevent an applet broadcasting your personal details to the Internet as a whole, or wiping your hard disk. ActiveX has no such restriction, so it is likely to be unpopular with system administrators.

Server push

As we will see in Chapter Eleven, when a web server delivers an HTML file, it begins with this header:

```
Content-type: text/html
```

The MIME standard for describing multimedia files allows a file to consist of multiple parts. These parts can either be different types of data (which is usually the case), or they can be sent one after another (which is what we want to do in this case).

You set up server push by producing a CGI script whose output is a multipart document. The script should put out one page, then pause for however long it wishes, put out the next page, and so on. Normally a server push script will keep putting out pages forever – the process is stopped when the user presses the "stop" button or stops looking at that page.

See Chapter Eleven for how to write CGI scripts.

The first thing the CGI script should print out is:

```
Content-type: mixed/x-mixed-replace;boundary=--TheEnd--
```

...and then two carriage returns. The "boundary=" bit tells the browser when a page of output is finished. Each time your script prints out "--TheEnd--" on a line by itself, the browser will display that page. You can have anything you like as the boundary line – it doesn't have to be

```
"--TheEnd--"
```

The script should then print out the page (which will have its own Content-type: line), and finish with the boundary line on its own. Then wait for a period, loop back, print another page, wait, print again, and so on.

A word of warning: many web space providers do not allow server push, because of the load it places on the server. Most web servers can only handle 5 or so connections at once. Normally, a connection only lasts for about a second, so many users can be handled at once. One server push connection can keep the connection up for minutes at a time. So if one user is looking at your site, it could be using up 20% of your entire site's resources for one page.

Client pull

Client pull is similar in some ways to server push, but it inflicts less load on the server. It works by adding an extra HTTP header to an HTML file which tells the browser to fetch the document (or a different document) again after a certain amount of time.

You can tell the server to add HTTP headers by putting a <META> tag in the HTML file's HEAD area. For example, if we add this tag to the HEAD:

```
<META HTTP-EQUIV="Refresh" CONTENT=1>
```

Then the browser will pretend that the document was sent with this HTTP header:

```
Refresh=1
```

This header tells the browser to fetch the document again after one second. If you made CONTENT equal to 25, it would wait 25 seconds.

The thing you really want to do is to fetch a *different* document. The header for this would look like this:

```
Refresh=1 ; URL=http://www.here.co.uk/file.html
```

The META tag for this would look like this:

```
<META HTTP-EQUIV="Refresh"
CONTENT="1 ; URL=http://www.here.co.uk/file.html">
```

You should try and put the whole tag on one line. The CONTENT attribute *must* all be one line.

The URL value you quote *must* be a fully-qualified URL – that is, with the "http://" part and all. Each of these headers is a "one-shot". The "Refresh" tag doesn't say "fetch this document every x seconds", it says "fetch this document, wait x seconds, and then fetch it again". That means that each file in a series of client pulls must have its own META tag.

There is one thing which client pull doesn't do, which it should. The Refresh header gives an absolute time after the file is displayed before refreshing. It doesn't allow a time for any images to load. If the connection is slow, the page will refresh while the pictures are still loading. It seems that there is no way round this.

Plug-ins

It has always been possible to provide files of any type from a web page. Files in formats which the web browser itself cannot handle would be handled by a helper application. Netscape's Plug-in technology allows you to handle unusual data formats more gracefully. Microsoft Internet Explorer also supports Plug-ins.

A plug-in is a program which links in with the browser. If the browser is asked to display data in a format which the Plug-in can handle, the plug-in takes over. The data is displayed as part of the HTML file displayed in the browser's window, just like an image.

Unless you are happy programming in C++, you can give up writing your own Plug-in. Fortunately, you won't need to. There are Plug-ins available for many useful data formats, and for some purposes there is a choice of Plug-ins to use. Often there is a free Plug-in to display data produced using a software package which you have to pay for. The best-known example of this is Shockwave, which displays files created with Macromedia Director.

You place Plug-in data on a page using the <EMBED> tag. This is very similar to an image tag, and can have these attributes:

SRC

The value of this attribute is the data you wish to display, just like the equivalent attribute for the IMG tag.

HEIGHT, WIDTH

These attributes give the size in pixels that the browser should reserve to display the Plug-in.

Most plug-ins also allow their own attributes to be defined: check the Plug-in's home page for details.

It is good manners to always put a link showing users where they can download particular Plug-ins. Note also that many Plug-ins are only available for people running the latest version of Windows, so not everyone will be able to see the full glory of your page.

Java

Oracle, Sun, IBM and Corel have joined forces to specify and develop the NC, but Microsoft and Intel will compete with a similar concept, the NetPC.

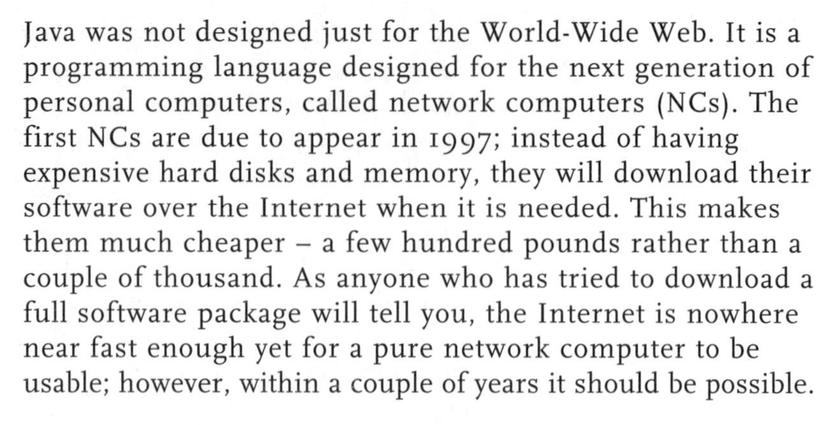

Java was not designed just for the World-Wide Web. It is a programming language designed for the next generation of personal computers, called network computers (NCs). The first NCs are due to appear in 1997; instead of having expensive hard disks and memory, they will download their software over the Internet when it is needed. This makes them much cheaper – a few hundred pounds rather than a couple of thousand. As anyone who has tried to download a full software package will tell you, the Internet is nowhere near fast enough yet for a pure network computer to be usable; however, within a couple of years it should be possible.

Java supports the concept of the network computer in a number of ways. Firstly, it is device-independent: a Java program will do the same thing regardless of the type of machine it is being run on. Secondly, the idea of a Java program being sent over a network, and possibly of parts of a program running on different machines, is fundamental to the language. There are security features built into the language which are supposed to stop a Java program from acting as a virus, damaging your hard disk, or copying personal information about you to a third party.

You can download the latest version of Java Development Kit (JDK) free from Sun Microsystems: http://java.sun.com

Its inventors, Sun, see Java as the language used by computers in a wide range of everyday objects: in years to come, they imagine computers running Java in your car, television, mobile phone and microwave oven. This would mean that you could set the video from anywhere in the world using your mobile phone, for example. We will have to wait and see whether this dream ever actually happens.

There is a special type of Java program, known as an "applet", which can be placed in an HTML page. It would take a complete book to teach you to write your own applets (and the language is changing so fast that by the time you read this book it would be out of date), but there are a wide variety of existing applets which you can download from the Internet and use on your pages.

Visual J++ is another implementation of Java produced by Microsoft.

The <APPLET> tag

You place an applet in an HTML document using the <APPLET> tag. This tag is a container – that is, it needs a start and an end tag. Within the tag, you can place one or more <PARAM> tags, which pass information to the applet, and HTML code which will be displayed by browsers which do not handle Java. This could be a description of the applet, or an image which shows what the applet should look like, or a link to an equivalent page which doesn't use Java.

The <APPLET> tag can have these attributes:

CODEBASE

This attribute gives the base URL where the code of the applet can be found – the URL of the folder in which the Java file is placed. If you do not use this attribute, the base URL of the current file is used.

CODE

This gives the name of the file of Java code. It is relative to the CODEBASE. Do not use an absolute URL.

ALT

This gives the text to display if the browser understands the <APPLET> tag, but cannot run a Java applet, for some reason.

NAME

This assigns a name to this instance of the applet. This allows applets displayed together on a page to pass information between them.

WIDTH, HEIGHT, ALIGN, VSPACE, HSPACE

These attributes have the same effects as the equivalent attributes of the <IMG> tag.

The <PARAM> tag is not a container. It has two attributes, NAME and VALUE, and is used to pass information to the applet. You can have as many or as few <PARAM> tags in an <APPLET> tag as you like.

JavaScript

In addition to supporting Java, Netscape have come up with a similar scripting language called "JavaScript". Whereas a Java applet is downloaded over the Internet, JavaScript is written into the web page. One advantage of this is that JavaScript often does not need an extra fetch from the server to have an effect: it will even work if it is part of a page saved to disk.

JavaScript code looks a lot like Java, but it is a much simpler language: in Java, for example, you can define your own "classes" of objects; JavaScript has a limited set of predefined objects and you are not able to add to this collection.

To write your own JavaScripts, you will need experience of programming; however there are archives of scripts on the Internet which you can include in your page.

You can use JavaScript in an HTML document in two ways. The first is to use the <SCRIPT> tag; the second method consists of attaching a call to a JavaScript routine to certain tags (for example form INPUT tags) which allow you to check the value entered before the form is submitted.

The <SCRIPT> tag

Between the <SCRIPT> tag and the </SCRIPT> tag, place lines of JavaScript. You can have as many sections of <SCRIPT> in an HTML document as you like. A good plan if you are defining JavaScript functions is to put them in a <SCRIPT> tag in the document's HEAD region – that way they are accessible anywhere in the document.

The SCRIPT tag can be used for languages other than JavaScript (as we will see). If this is likely to be a problem, you can add a LANGUAGE attribute to the tag, to tell the browser which language the script is written in.

Adding JavaScript handlers to tags

You can add an attribute to certain types of HTML tag which will run some JavaScript code when an "Event" occurs. An event is a thing which the user does – it includes "Focus" (selecting a field, so that the text cursor appears), "Blur" (nothing to do with Britpop – it's when the focus goes away from an object), "MouseOver" (moving the mouse over an object), and so on.

It is possible to write the JavaScript code directly in the tag, but it's usually better to define a JavaScript routine in a <SCRIPT> tag in the HEAD of the document, and then make a call to this routine. For example, suppose that we have defined a JavaScript routine "ping()" (which makes a sound) in the HEAD section of an HTML document. Then we can use this notation:

```
<A HREF=somewhere onMouseOver="ping()">...
```

...and every time you point the mouse at that anchor, the routine is run.

These are the events that JavaScript can recognise, and the tags to which you can apply them:

Focus, Blur, Change	Text inputs, Textareas, Select fields
Click	Radio buttons, checkboxes, submit and reset inputs, Anchors
Select	Text inputs, Textareas
MouseOver	Anchors

The name of the attribute to add to a tag for a particular event is the name of the event with "on" added to the front. That is: to set up a handler of Change events, use the attribute "onChange=...".

ActiveX

ActiveX is Microsoft's answer to Plug-ins and Java (although Internet Explorer can handle these as well). An ActiveX "component" is downloaded from the remote server if necessary, and then acts just like a Plug-in. You can add scripting to an HTML document in either VBScript (Visual Basic scripting edition) or JScript (Microsoft's implementation of JavaScript).

The thing that makes ActiveX different is that it is a development of Microsoft's OLE technology, which is what you use when you paste a section of an Excel spreadsheet into a Word document. This means that a Word or Excel file can be an ActiveX component, and that you can paste ActiveX Plug-ins into Office97 applications. If you're running Windows, that is (and all the people who look at your page are running Windows too). There is a Netscape Plug-in which allows you to run ActiveX components in Netscape Navigator, as well as Internet Explorer, but otherwise only Internet Explorer users will be able to see your components.

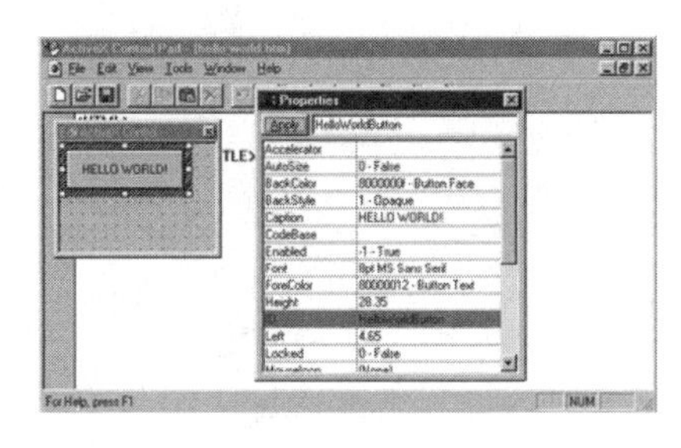

You can place ActiveX components into an HTML document using the <OBJECT> tag, which has almost the same syntax as the <APPLET> tag (in fact, there is talk of using <OBJECT> for all of these types of in-line objects – applets, plug-ins, images, and so on). Microsoft provide you with a free software application, ActiveX Control Pad, which allows you to place these objects directly on the page in an interactive, what-you-see-is-what-you-get manner. You can download the Control Pad from Microsoft's page:

http://www.microsoft.com/workshop/author/cpad

HANDY TIP

To look at sample pages using ActiveX Controls look at: http://www.microsoft.com/activex/controls.

CHAPTER ELEVEN

CGI

The Common Gateway Interface allows you to use the output of a program, rather than HTML files, to provide pages. This chapter describes the essentials of CGI scripting, and suggests some tools which may be of use.

Covers

How CGI works

There are many things you could want to do on a web site which you cannot do using HTML alone, but which can be handled by a program running on the host computer. Examples of this could include:

- Getting information about a particular visitor;
- Fetching pictures from a camera or other device;
- Producing dynamically-changing information (stock quotes, sports results, etc.)
- Handling the information given by fill-in forms (see Chapter Seven)
- Implementing image maps (see Chapter Five)

REMEMBER **Forms and image maps are covered in their own chapters.**

All these functions can be handled using the Common Gateway Interface, or CGI for short.

In brief, CGI works as follows: when asked for a CGI link the server, instead of sending a file, runs a program. The output of this program is then returned just as if it were an HTML file, and the browser on the other end is none the wiser.

CGI "scripts" are simply short programs; the only restriction is that they are non-interactive – they take a series of command-line arguments, run, and produce a result with no other intervention (so you can't run Doom as a CGI script). Otherwise, anything is possible: a CGI script can return HTML, a GIF image, or anything else the browser can handle.

To produce a CGI script from scratch, you have to be able to program. The actual details of programming are beyond the scope of this book, so we'll concentrate on how to integrate the CGI script with the rest of a web site.

Suitable scripting languages

In principle, a CGI script can be written in any programming language which can be run on the computer on which the server is running. In practice, there are a few limitations.

The first restriction comes from the fact that nothing is returned by the server until the CGI script has finished running. If the server does not send a reply within a few seconds of receiving a request, the browser on the other end may assume that it's not running, and give up. For this reason, your CGI script needs to finish in as short a time as possible, so it needs to run quickly and can't try and do anything too elaborate. This requirement usually means that .BAT files will be too slow, as will Windows-based programs or fancy things like databases.

The second restriction is because often you don't have exclusive charge of the computer on which the server is running. Whoever is in charge of the computer will take a dim view of a program which they can't examine being run by anyone on the Internet. For this reason, if you want to use a program in a compiled language such as C or FORTRAN, they will usually want to check it out first. This may prove expensive in fees the server owner will charge to cover the costs of checking and installing the program. If you own the computer, then fine, use C or C++, but otherwise, you'll have to use an interpreted language. Most commercial web servers run on Unix machines, as well, so Visual Basic is out, too.

You can download PERL from http://www.perl.com/perl/.

For a combination of the above reasons, the commonest language for CGI scripts (and my personal favourite) is PERL. PERL is interpreted, which means that the system administrators can check your code; it's fast running, and very good at the sort of data-shifting that you need for a CGI script; there are versions available for almost all types of computers. Oh yes, and it's free.

PERL

PERL (which stands for "Practical Extraction and Report Language") was invented by an American systems programmer called Larry Wall when he wanted an easy and quick language for Unix systems programming. Fortunately, he put the resulting program on the Internet, where other people contributed and improved, and today there is a full programming environment available for free to anyone with Internet access. You can find the files you'll need to program in PERL, along with with plenty of information about the language, at:

The only thing you do pay for is Larry's two books, "Learning PERL" and "Programming in PERL", which are highly recommended.

http://www.perl.com/perl/

If you've ever programmed in C or C++ then PERL will look very familiar. It's not that far from Unix "shell" programming or DOS .BAT scripts, either. Like BAT files, a PERL script runs straight away – C has to first be "compiled" to produce an executable file, which is then run. PERL compiles a program when it is run, which gives it most of the speed of a C program, but the ease of development of a .BAT file or a BASIC program.

Like a proper grown-up computer language, PERL allows you full access to the innards of your computer, and on the Internet you can find a wide range of "libraries" of subroutines to add to your programs – for example, there is a complete web server written in PERL, and all the code is available for you to use.

Passing information to a script

Many CGI scripts do not need information supplied to them – they just run and produce a result. Other scripts need information supplied by the server or by the user. The most common case of this is with fill-in forms, which were discussed in Chapter Seven. Otherwise the procedure is as follows:

When a CGI script is called, any extra data to send to the script is encoded in the URL. The extra data is separated from the rest of the URL by a "?" sign. In addition, any spaces in the data are converted to "+" signs, and any other non-alphanumeric characters are replaced by "%xy", where "xy" is the hexadecimal ascii code for that character. So, to run a CGI script called "print" with the parameter "Hello World", the URL would be:

http://www.mysite.co.uk/cgi-bin/print?Hello+World

From the CGI script's point of view, everything in the URL after the first "?" is stored in the environment variable QUERY_STRING. It's up to you to decode any character substitutions which have taken place.

If your script is written in PERL, you may find the library **cgi-lib** useful. You can find the library, and full documentation, at:

http://www.bio.cam.ac.uk/cgi-lib/

The output of a script

Anything output by a script is processed by the http server, and sent back to the browser which requested the link. In this respect, a CGI script is a bit like the simple programs you write when you first learn to program – it takes various bits of information, rearranges them a bit, and then prints it all out neatly. Of course, that's not all the script can do – it can update files, send an eMail, and so on. But a CGI script should always return *something*. If it returns nothing, the user will see "Document returned no data", which doesn't just look like an error, it *is* an error.

There are two sorts of thing a CGI script can return: data of some type (usually HTML or an image), or a link to an existing page, which the server will return.

Returning a location

If you want your script to return an existing page, all your page should print out is:

```
Location: http://www.somesite.co.uk/location.html
```

The browser will then fetch the URL you have specified.

Returning an HTML document

To return an HTML document (or any other type of data) you need to print two things: a header which defines the type of data to follow (in this case HTML), and the HTML code for the page. You can put whatever HTML features you like in the document body, even other links to CGI scripts.

The data header

If you don't include a header, the browser will assume it is receiving a text file, and will display it in a fixed font, mark-up and all. Plain text can't have anchors, so that would leave the user with nowhere else to go except press the back button.

The data header should be the first thing printed out by your script. It must begin with "Content-type:", followed by a space, followed by a description of the type of data, followed by two line breaks. Don't, whatever you do, forget the two line breaks: if you only use one, the header will not be recognised, and you will spend hours trying to work out why your script doesn't work.

The description of the type of data follows a format known as "MIME" which is the Internet standard for describing multiple types of data. You encounter MIME in a couple of other places in connection with the World-Wide Web: in choosing helper applications, and in setting up a fill-in form for file upload.

A MIME descriptor consists of two words divided by a slash, "/". The first word describes the general type of data which follows; the second defines the exact format. For example, HTML has a MIME type of "text/html". A GIF file has MIME type "image/gif".

BEWARE

Don't forget the two line breaks!

So, the header for an HTML file should be:

```
Content-type: text/html
```

The content of the document

The rest of the output of your CGI script should be the HTML code to be displayed. This part of your script just consists of lots of print commands printing the HTML which you require.

It takes a bit of thought to write a program which will output HTML to make a particular page, but you can do anything that you can do in normal HTML in the output of a CGI script – images, forms, other CGI scripts, whatever you like.

Implementing CGI

Once you've written and debugged your CGI script, you need to install it on your World-Wide Web server. In particular, it's important that the server knows that the script should be run, rather than just returned like any other file. Depending on the type of server, there are two conventions for placing CGI files.

The older method, which many servers still use, is to specify one or more directories to be a "CGI binaries" directory. Any file in this directory will be assumed to be a script, and if accessed, the file will be run. Often there is a server alias set up to allow this directory to be easily addressed in URLs.

If your server uses this method, you will be given the name of a directory in which to put your scripts. This directory is often called "cgi-bin". You will be told the path to put in a URL to access scripts in this directory. Usually, this is "/ cgi-bin/". So, imagine you have a CGI script which returns a GIF image of the current time, which is called "time". You place this file in your cgi-bin directory, and then you can include this image in a page by inserting the mark-up:

You could also use /cgi-bin/ time as the HREF of a link. This would display the time when you click on the link.

```
<IMG SRC="/cgi-bin/time">
```

The easier way of designating a CGI script is the one used by the Netscape server. In this case, if a file to be fetched is executable, the server will treat it as a CGI file: if not, it returns the file. So, if PERL files on your server machine end with ".pl", any files on your server which end in ".pl" will be assumed to be PERL files and will be run as a CGI file. This is much easier to handle than just having one CGI directory. Note that a site set up for the other type of server will also work under the Netscape server – all the CGI files just happen to be in a directory called "cgi-bin".

CHAPTER TWELVE

Anatomy of a Web Site

This chapter explains how the World-Wide Web works, and looks at the mechanics of setting up your site.

Covers

World-Wide Web servers

Programs which run constantly are sometimes referred to as "daemons" after the creatures in Greek mythology who made things work. The Christian word "demon" is derived from this, but daemons didn't have horns or carry tridents.

When you use a web browser to request a World-Wide Web page, your browser sends a request to a World-Wide Web Server at the remote site. The term "server" is used in two ways: for the machine which stores the web pages, and for a special program which runs constantly on that machine, handling requests and sending files when asked.

A single World-Wide Web page will usually consist of a single file of HyperText Markup Language (HTML for short), plus one graphics file for each different image on the page. Each file has to be requested and sent separately, so fetching a complete web page will often require a number of connections between your browser and the remote server. This is a good reason to keep the number of different images on a page to as few as you can.

A server is set up with a set area of disk space on its host computer, where it finds the files for it to deliver. You construct a site by putting files in this area of disk space.

A server can do a number of things other than just deliver files, which will be explained as we need them. One of the more interesting things servers do is keep a log of each file that is fetched. This allows you to look at our web site and see who's been looking at your site, when they've looked it, which files are most popular, and so on.

There are a number of different server programs available. Since they differ in subtle (but quite important) ways, you should make sure that you know exactly which server is handling a web site which you're building.

The NCSA Server

The first web server was written at the National Center for Supercomputer Applications in Illinois (the people who produced Mosaic). It is viewed as the baseline against which everything else is assessed, which unfortunately means that it's not really that impressive.

The main advantage of the NCSA server is that since it was developed as a research project it's completely free and there's a lot of information available – even program source code. You'll still find the NCSA server in use at academic sites, but most commercial sites go for something more sexy.

Apache

The Apache server was designed as a souped-up version of the NCSA server. It's also freely available, and is faster than NCSA as well as having a few extra features useful in a commercial site, such as better security. You'll find that quite a few commercial sites run Apache, notably Demon Internet.

CERN

The CERN server was designed as an alternative to the NCSA server, and improves on it in a number of ways. In particular, a machine running CERN can also act as a web proxy, improving access times to distant sites for local users. However, CERN pales against more recent commercial programs.

Netscape

Netscape corporation produce a range of web servers which are state-of-the-art for commercial sites. They have been written to run fast and to easily handle a large number of simultaneous requests, and they are very easy to administer, because you set them up using a World-Wide Web interface. The top model, the Commerce Server, will run secure links to suitable web browsers, allowing things like credit card numbers to be entered safely.

The big problem with the Netscape servers is that they are commercial packages, and thus cost money – in the case of the Commerce Server, several thousand pounds. However, if you want a really top-class web site, you should insist on the best.

Other servers

All the servers described so far run on computers running the Unix operating system, which is what you will find most commercial web servers will use.

There are other options. Microsoft produce web servers which run on Windows NT or even on a Windows machine. There is also a server which runs on a PowerPC Apple Macintosh. These have the advantage of not needing Unix skills to administer the server, and some of them are used commercially – Microsoft's own servers run under Windows NT, and The Guardian's server runs on Apples.

The main use of these servers (assuming you can't afford a leased line to your home or office) is that you can prototype a complete web server, test it and demonstrate it, without having to put it on the Internet, where other people can look at your incomplete efforts. This really speeds up the development process.

Your own server?

There are two ways to put a web site on the World-Wide Web. You can either run your own server, or you can rent space on a commercial web server.

The approach of having your own server sounds appealing initially. You own the equipment, so you adjust it whenever you want, and you are quite free to upgrade it any time you want, to allow for demand. With the exception of very ambitious projects, however, you will find it too expensive an option.

A busy web site can place a significant load on the machine it's running on. For this reason, it's usually best to have a dedicated machine which is doing little if anything else. This machine needs to run a multi-tasking operating system, so a Windows NT machine is the absolute minimum – a Unix machine would be better. Running a Unix system takes a level of skill a long way beyond the scope of this book, so unless you feel confident with Unix don't even consider it.

Then you have to consider the matter of the connection to the Internet. A web server needs to be accessible from the rest of the Internet at any time. In practice, this will mean either a leased-line or an ISDN connection for your server. This means a cost of at least £5,000 per year just for the connection, almost certainly more. In any case, a dial-up connection will definitely not be sufficient.

The one perk of buying a server on a leased line is that you can connect all the other machines in the vicinity more-or-less for free – possibly a good idea if you're setting up a site for a company with a large number of PCs all of which need Internet access. However, unless an investment of £20,000-£30,000 per year doesn't set you back, you're better off going for Plan B...

Buying web space

The solution for most of us is to rent space on a commercial World-Wide Web server. Most Internet Service Providers run a World-Wide Web server, and most of them are willing to rent out disk space on the server to the public. The cost varies, but is usually a few pounds per megabyte per month. Many Service Providers offer a small amount of space (usually half a megabyte or so) for free to each of their subscribers. You can fit quite a nice personal web site in half a megabyte.

It's worth shopping around before you settle on a particular company to place your site on. Web space is now so cheap that cost is rarely an issue. Check which server the site runs – Netscape sites tend to be more expensive, but it can be worth the extra. Find out about how you put files on the server – there are subtle differences between different servers, and some are more easy than others. In particular, check the performance of the site. Look at web sites which are already there, to see how quickly the server responds. If you can, check the server from different providers – if you've got a contact abroad, ask them to try the server and tell you what they think.

You can find a list of companies offering web space rental at http://www.yahoo.com

Remember, you don't have to use a web server which is physically near to you. In principle your server can be anywhere on the Internet. American sites, in particular, tend to be cheaper than UK ones, and most of them have *really* nice connectivity.

Layout of a web site

"Directory Tree" is the term used in Unix for a folder which contains other folders, which contain other folders, and so on.

A web site is stored on its host computer as a directory tree. When you set up the World-Wide Web server, you specify a directory called the "server root". Nothing outside of this directory tree will be visible over the web – you wouldn't want hackers looking around your computer's system files, etc. For speed, it's best if the server root is stored on a local disk to the server (and on a fast disk if possible), but in principle it could be stored on a disk on a file server, or anywhere else accessible from the server machine. I'm not suggesting that you place a web site on a floppy disk, but it's possible.

You can either put the whole of your web site in a single directory, or put different sections in their own directory – it's up to you, but it's easier to handle a large site if you use multiple directories.

Each directory must at least have a home page, called "index.html". This is the first place visited in a site, or in an area of a site. This page can have links to other pages, or to graphics. Each graphic is a file, usually in .GIF or .JPEG format. It's up to you whether you put graphics files in the same directory as the HTML file which refers to them, or if you have a special directory just for graphics.

Designing your site

It doesn't really matter whether you use a visual HTML editor, or whether you just use a text editor to produce your pages: the basic procedure is the same. Put the HTML files and graphic files in a set of folders on your hard disk which mimics the way they will be laid out on the server machine. Even if you have your own server, it's a good idea to get the site right before you put it on-line – you don't want other people stumbling across your pages before they're perfect, do you?

Under Windows 3.1, you will need to run Trumpet WinSock to allow Netscape to run. You *don't* need to be dialled in, however.

If you're using a text editor to produce your pages, you can use a web browser such as Netscape to view your pages as you work on them. Just use the "Open File" command of Netscape to fetch a page from your local disk rather than from the Internet. Assuming you have enough memory to run both your editor and Netscape, you can switch from one to the other, making changes and seeing what effect they have as you go along.

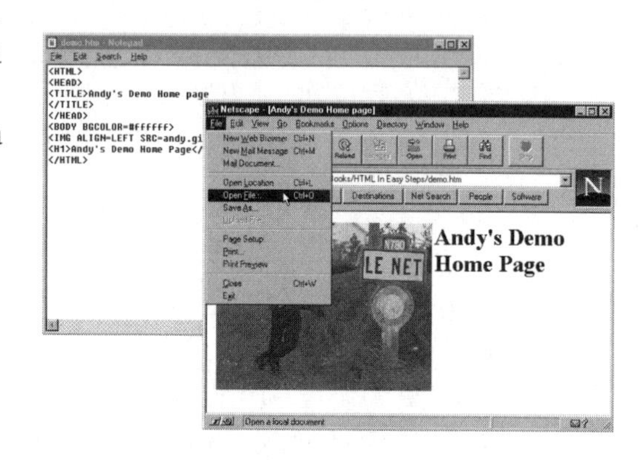

If you don't know where to start on your web page, here's a tip: HTML is an interpreted language – that is, it is possible to look at any web site on the Internet and see how it's done. So: spend a little time browsing the web, and when you find a page that you like, save it onto your local disk. After a while you will have a collection of HTML files which you can edit as you like to produce your web site. It's always easier to get going when you have a framework to work from.

Even if you use a specialised HTML editor to prepare your pages, it is still a good idea to try out your service before it goes live. In particular, check that all the links on your pages work: it's very easy to mistype a file name and so leave a broken link. It's a good idea to ask someone else to check your pages for you, since that will usually find any problems.

You can test most features of a service without running a web server. The big exception to this is CGI scripts, or features which rely on them, such as forms or server-side image maps. You may have to test these on the final site, since it can be very difficult to fully reproduce the setup on the real web server. You can do a lot of testing, however, by running a web server on your computer, and fetching pages from that. There are freeware web servers available for a wide range of personal computers (there's even one which runs under MS-DOS).

CGI scripts are covered in Chapter 11.

Here's a handy trick to speed up server response if you're lucky enough to have more than one machine linked over a LAN: if the server is running on the same computer as the browser which is examining the pages, you will get a slower performance than you should, because whenever the server has to respond to a request, the machine is already busy (the browser is making a request...). If you can place the server on one machine and fetch the pages with another you will get a much better performance. It even works if people are developing on both machines at once: run a server on each machine, and use each other's servers.

Installing your site

Once you have written your site, and you're satisfied with it, you need to copy the files onto the web. If you are lucky enough to have your own server, this is easy – just copy the files into the correct location. If not, then you have to put the files on your provider's web site.

It is just possible that a provider will let you send them a floppy disk – but if they will, they will definitely charge you for the privilege. The normal way of installing the files is using FTP.

FTP is short for "File Transfer Protocol". It is an Internet service which allows you to copy files to and from the Internet. Most people use FTP to download software from archive sites: this is one of the few times that you will use FTP to upload files.

When you arrange your web space with your provider, they will give you a number of items of information:

- The Internet address to FTP to
- The location on this site of your server
- Your username
- Your password

You will need a program called an FTP client to do FTP. There are a number of these available on the Internet. Pretty much all of them are freeware or shareware, so all you have to do is download them and install them.

You can download WS FTP from http://www.shareware.com.

One particularly good FTP client is WS FTP. There is a version of WS FTP for Windows 3.1, and a 32-bit version for Windows 95 or NT. If you can run the 32-bit version then do so – it runs a lot more smoothly.

It is worth setting up a WS FTP profile for your web site – this avoids having to type in passwords every time.

1. Select the "New" button of the profile window, and type in a title for your site

2. Fill in the FTP address, username and password (your provider will tell you this)

3. It will save time if you fill in the initial directories for the FTP site and for where you have put the files for your site

Once you have set up WS FTP, here is how to install your site:

1. Dial into your Internet Provider

2. Connect using the FTP profile we have just set up

3. Select all the files you wish to send to the site (usually this will be all of them)

4. Press the "send" button

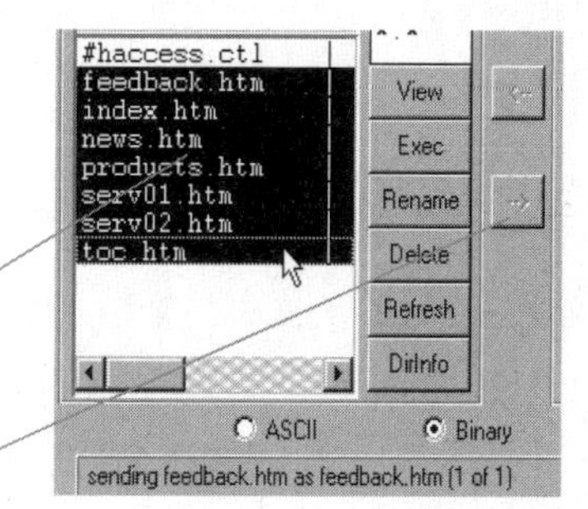

This is the procedure for most Internet Service Providers. On a few of them, such as Demon Internet, you have to FTP the files up and then use Telnet to connect to their machine and copy the files into the correct position.

Tips when uploading files

Firstly, be patient. This is probably the biggest upload you've done up to now, and it can be surprising how long it can take. As an estimate, a 14.4 modem can transfer about 1K per second (HTML files will go faster than images, since the modems can compress the data as it's going over the telephone link). That means that a megabyte of data will take just over 17 minutes to upload – more than you would originally think. It seems a *lot* longer when you're sitting watching the modem lights flicker.

If you are still using Windows 3.1, be careful about file names. If you FTP a file called INDEX.HTM onto a Unix machine (which is what the server probably runs) it will probably come out as "index.htm" – or it may not, depending on the FTP server on your provider. web servers can tell the difference between a link to "index.htm" and one to "INDEX.HTM". This can make your links stop working when you put it on the server. All you can do is to be careful about the problem, and watch in case it occurs. If it does, you may have to alter your HTML files.

This problem will go away if you use Windows 95 (or if you use a Macintosh), but another problem appears. Both these operating systems allow spaces in file names. Unix systems can have spaces in file names, but it causes all sorts of problems. Avoid using spaces in file names. If you really want multi-word names for your files, use an underline "_" instead of spaces.

Advertising your pages

Once your pages are in place, you have the problem of letting people know that your pages are on the Net. If you don't advertise them, nobody will visit them.

If your page is just a personal home page, or if it covers a special interest of yours, all you need to do is to tell the people that you know on the Internet to look at it. If you can find any pages on the same or a similar subject, then let the author know – they are usually keen to include a link to related pages as long as you are willing to include a link to them on your pages in return.

This advice is, to a certain degree, worth following for a commercial site, especially for a small specialist company and if you provide information other than a straight sales pitch. Obviously there's no point in asking competitors to link to your site! The main place to advertise a commercial site is on various search engines and listing sites.

There are now dozens of search engines on the web, and more are being added all the time. A few of them run special programs to search the web and add sites automatically, but most of them require you to submit an entry for your site, usually with some additional information about what is found there and in which categories it should be placed. There is generally a web page to do this. Once you have submitted your details, the owners of the site will vet your entry, making sure that it is appropriate (and that it works!) and will then put it on their server. This usually takes a few weeks to come into effect.

It would be easy to spend a couple of hours on-line submitting your site on various search engines, and you would probably still miss a few. There are now a number of services on the web which allow you to enter your details once, and they then submit your site to a number of different search engines for you. A number of these are a free service: others charge for the privilege.

The first submission service, and probably the most complete, is called Submit It!, and while it provides a limited service for free, for complete coverage you have to register and pay a fee. This costs about $50 for a year's subscription – during that time you can register other sites for free.

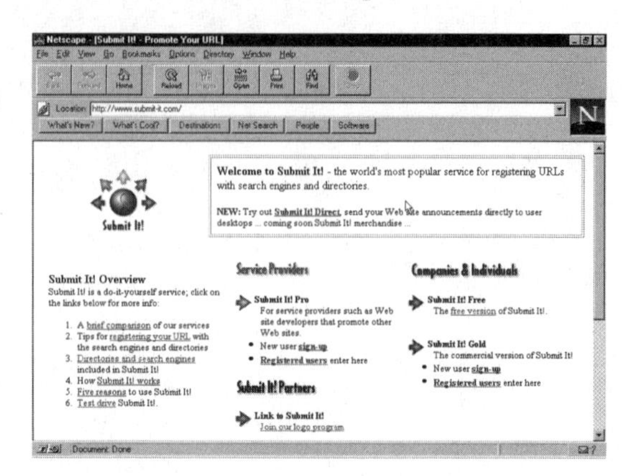

Submit-It is entirely accessed via its web pages. To access it, point your web browser at:

http://www.submit-it.com

From there, you can apply for an account (if you pay by credit card, you can then go straight on and use your account).

You supply all the information necessary about your site using a fill-in form. There is some basic information that you have to supply for all sites (like the URL of the site, and your contact details), and then there is a series of sections for notable index sites which require their own particular information. At the end of this process (which takes about 20 minutes to work through) you simply press the "submit" button and Submit-It goes off and registers your site with over 200 index sites world-wide (you can specify any sites with which you don't want to be registered).

When your entry appears on the destination site is up to the index sites themselves; Submit-It has no control over this, but it is one step along the road.

CHAPTER THIRTEEN

Limiting Access to Your Server

There are occasions when you want to restrict who can access a page on your server. This chapter explains how to set this up.

Covers

Introduction

From time to time you need to restrict who can access your pages. There are a number of cases in which you would wish to do this.

One case is when you have a server which has information which needs to be updated frequently. You can avoid having to upload a new HTML file every time this information is changed by setting up a form which allows you to enter information which is then incorporated into the page. Obviously you would not want anyone on the Internet to be able to get to this page: ideally only you (or the person who will do the updates) will be able to get to it.

Another case would be if you have information on a server for which you wish to charge. Certain parts of your site are available to all, but to get to the private areas a user needs to give a password.

A third case is if you are setting up an intranet for a company or an organization, which carries confidential company information. Only computers in that company should be allowed to access these pages.

HTTP servers allow you to limit access to areas of your server to people who provide a username and a password (you can have as many usernames and passwords as you like). You can also limit access according to the Internet address from which the page is being fetched. You can either allow access from particular addresses (or from a particular domain), and you can ban access from particular addresses or domains.

One limit on this that you should bear in mind is that many public Internet Service Providers use what is called "dynamic address allocation". The company has a pool of Internet addresses for its customer accounts, and each time a particular customer dials in, they are given an address from this pool, for this connection only. If a machine is directly connected to the Internet, it will always have the same address.

The .htaccess file

The method described in this chapter is that used by NCSA and CERN servers, and by servers based on these programs. The Netscape server uses its own system which can do the same things, but is more complicated.

REMEMBER **The file must be called ".htaccess" (with the dot at the beginning). This is how Unix hides files.**

Access to files in any particular directory on a web server is controlled by a file called ".htaccess" in the directory. If there is no .htaccess file in a directory, then anyone can access the files in that directory. If there is a .htaccess file, then access permission for all files in that directory and in all subdirectories of that directory is dependent on the contents of the file. You can of course have different .htaccess files in different directories.

The .htaccess file consists of two parts:

- Headers, which give the address of password files and such like;
- A <LIMIT> tag

The .htaccess headers

The header section of the .htaccess file consists of a number of lines. It should look a bit like this:

AuthUserFile */otherdir/.htpasswd*
AuthGroupFile */otherdir/.htgroup*
AuthName *ByPassword*
AuthType *Basic*

The part of each line in *italics* is the bit that you can alter for your purposes. Going through the headers in order:

AuthUserFile

The value of this header should be the exact Unix pathname of your password file. You do not have to have a password file in the same place as your HTML files – in fact it's better if you hide it away somewhere. Check with your provider for the best place to put your password file. This file will be discussed at the end of this chapter.

AuthGroupFile

The value of this header should be the exact Unix pathname of your group file, if you have one. The group file allows you to collect a number of usernames together into a group, and allow or deny access to all of them in a single line. If you don't want a group file, set this header to "/dev/null".

AuthName

When someone tries to access a file in this directory, your browser will ask them "Please give username and password for *xxxxx*", where *xxxxx* is the value of this header. It's also remembered by the browser so you don't have to give the password for every file in this area.

AuthType

This tells the server and browser how to encode the access information which the user provides. "Basic" is the simplest (and least secure) method, but it always works. There are other types available, which your server may handle. The only way to find out is to ask your provider.

The <LIMIT> tag

The rest of the .htaccess file should consist of a <LIMIT> tag (it could consist of more than one, but you rarely need to do this). The <LIMIT> tag is a container – it has a start and an end tag. The tag can have any or all of the three attributes which determine which actions this tag affects. The attributes are:

GET

This <LIMIT> tag affects http GET actions – that is, fetching HTML documents etc.

PUT

This <LIMIT> tag affects whether files can be put in this directory. You will almost never need to use this.

POST

This <LIMIT> tag affects whether scripts and forms can be run in this directory.

The <LIMIT> tag can contain one or more lines which describe the conditions for accessing files in this directory. Possible lines are:

order allow,deny *or* order deny,allow

This line describes whether the permission should be interpreted to mean "allow, except for..." or "deny, except for..."

deny from ...
allow from ...

These lines either allow or deny access depending on the Internet address from which the request is coming. The value at the end can either be "all", which is a blanket permission or denial except as amended by later lines, or an Internet address. The address can be a complete domain name, or just a part of a domain: "allow .uk" will allow access from any site whose address ends with "uk", "deny .ac.uk" will deny access from any UK academic site, and so on. Finally, you can put in the numerical address, if you want to.

require user *fred*

The user will be asked for a username and a password. They must give "fred" as the username, and give fred's password, as set up in the password file.

require group *friends*

The user will be asked for a username and a password. They must give a username which is defined as being in the group "friends" in the group file, and give the correct password for that user according to the password file.

The group and password files

If you are setting up authorisation by password, you need to set up a password file, and optionally a group file.

The password file is usually called ".htpasswd" – though you can choose anything you like. You only have to have one password file, and all your .htaccess files can use the same one, if you want to.

You will probably have to connect to your provider's computer using a telnet program, since to set the file up you have to use a program called "htpasswd" on the server machine. This is (roughly) what you should type once you are connected to your server computer:

```
% htpasswd -c .htpasswd andy
```

htpasswd	-c	.htpasswd	andy
This is the name of the htpasswd program	The "-c" tells the program to create a new password file, if this is your first time	The .htpasswd is the name of the password file to use	"andy" is the username which you wish to add

The program will then ask you to type the password for that user, and to repeat it, to make sure that you haven't mistyped it.

The group file is simpler, and you can produce it on your own computer. It consists of a series of lines, one for each group. Each line should look like this:

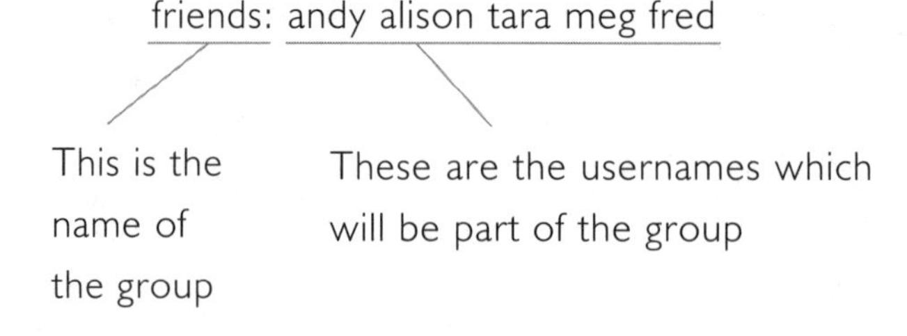

Index

A

B

C

D

E

M

N

O

P

Q

R

S

T

U

V

W